THE SOUTHERN WA

C000225674

CONTENTS

© Kevin Robertson (Noodle Books) and the various contributors 2014
ISBN 978-1-909328-18-1
First published in 2014 by Kevin Robertson
under the **NOODLE BOOKS** imprint
PO Box 279
Corhampton
SOUTHAMPTON
SO32 3ZX
www.noodlebooks.co.uk
editorial@thesouthernway.co.uk

Printed in England by
Berforts Information Press Ltd.

Above - And now for something completely different..... . Colour images in 'SW' are nothing new, but this page displays a new departure for us and one upon which I will be interested to hear views upon. The subject matter may be obvious, but just in case it depicts 'L12' No 433 but attached to the tender of 'D15' No 468: very confusing for the mature spotters on the left, who are dressed in suitably old fashioned garb. This photograph was taken at Eastleigh on 28 August 1938 with both locomotive and tender seen here in the Maunsell shade of dark green. The original image is from a very sharp medium/large format negative on which the numberplate of the 'L12' can also be read. Also on this page is 'O2' No 14 'Fishbourne' standing in the bay platform at Brading with a Bembridge branch train sometime between 1948 and 1953. Colour from this period is rare and so the chances of finding anything of this clarity are always welcome. However, and here comes the interesting point, these scenes started life as conventional b/w images which have been expertly coloured by David P Williams. My own perspective is that this is little different to decades past when our Victorian and Edwardian forebears would hand-tint a postcard. The advantage nowadays being that we now have the opportunity to go one step further thanks to modern computer graphics programmes. Of course the opposite side of the coin would be for someone to say the colour is wrong. (Do not criticise the actual photographs because they are 100% genuine.) To counter the critic I would respond with, "try matching something of your own at home with the exact same shade in the supermarket". The same applies when we look at colour photographs from past years reproduced in a book or magazine. Is the colour truly as it appeared or has the image faded or is the reproduction less than the best that might be achieved? You will gather I am quite taken with the whole idea, opening up as is does a whole new field for the historian, not just for locomotives but rolling stock, stations etc, in fact the complete railway vista. Because it is so different it needs to be done well (as here) but I will also admit it is a field that needs careful thought but one where we can combine the advantages of modern technology to present the past literally in a new light. I would welcome comments. (With grateful thanks to David P Williams for allowing his images to be used in this way.)

Opposite page - Near the end of its working life, No 34099 minus its 'Lynmouth' nameplate on a p/way working at Guildford.

Editorial

Wearing one of several hats (publisher, enthusiast, reader, writer, researcher, interviewer), I have become used to reading accounts by railwaymen of their exploits, usually speaking from an operational perspective. What I often find fascinating in these accounts is the working conditions that were endured, cold, long hours and basically hard-labour - without it seems much chance of remission for good conduct! As such it is tempting to believe that those 'higher up the food chain' might well have enjoyed an opposite lifestyle and indeed, depending on how far up the tree an individual sat, that could well have been the case.

Receiving what we are placing as our lead article for this issue is something which perhaps destroys the illusion that management enjoyed the 'cushy' life. What I think also makes this a little different is that the recollections are recorded, not by the actual railwayman but instead his daughter, and who was therefore able to witness first-hand the conditions endured and difficulties faced. If this makes the Southern seem a harsh and uncaring employer then think again. It would have been no different on the GWR, LMS or LNER, these were the working circumstances of the time, 'take it or leave it'. As a record of the life of a manager in a past generation it is a worthy testimony.

We are delighted also to continue the series of the history of the Southern Railway with Alan Blackburn (co-author of the OPC 'Southern Wagons' series of books) having taken up the challenge from the late Tony Goodyear. As Alan put it to me when he agreed to the task, he did not feel it appropriate to continue in exactly the same form as

Tony and in consequence has put his own spin on the series which I also think fits well. Like Tony, Alan was a professional railwayman and we must never forget that seeing things from the opposite side of the fence will naturally result in a different perspective to that of the enthusiast. I am glad that in his text Alan has been prepared to discuss areas previously sacrosanct. You may not always agree but we should never just look at history through rose-tinted spectacles.

Also in this issue is a major work by John Atkinson and Colin Watts on the Southern 2-BIL units. For long part of the Southern Railway/Region scene, I always felt they fitted in so well, that is until the day corporate blue arrived. From that time on they (and indeed every SR built unit) aged overnight and it was perhaps even better to see them disappear and instead recall their heyday rather than accept what I still believe was a railway becoming ever more bland as time passed.

Finally a request. We have been shown a potential manuscript prepared sometime prior to March 1994 by **Mr Philip Green of Farnham.** We have attempted to contact Mr Green at the address current at the time but without success. If anyone has any leads on this person we would be most grateful

As always, thank you all for your continued support. I am delighted to report the pile of material for future use hardly seems to diminish. Be assured I have no wish to see the blotter uncovered whilst even more drawers (and computer hard-drives) can be acquired, so please keep up with the submissions.

Kevin Robertson

Front cover - *The preserved LSWR T3, No 563 at Brighton.*
Pages 2/3 - *The unmistakable vista of Worting Junction west of Basingstoke. This is the point where the Southern West of England route curves away from the Bournemouth line - the latter down line may be seen on the extreme left. The up Bournemouth line crosses the West of England on the flyover and where both lines meet it is then four track all the way to Waterloo. The (fitted?) freight hualed by a 'U' class Mogul is heading towards Salisbury.* *Henry Meyer*
Rear cover - *'I don't believe it', as Victor Meldrew might well have said. This image was submitted by Colin Watts who has come up with the comment that the ramps are probably there to keep a wet hose from shorting the track-circuiting, but then surely showing the line as occupied would have been a good idea. But it is NOT on the SR - or indeed in the UK!*

Above - *Unidentified 'King Arthur' outside Eastbourne shed in 1932 - notice the vacuum pump under the crosshead. Roy's career took him here two years later in 1934.*

Left - *Roy Steele, 1905 - 1968. Southern Railway 1923 - 1947 and Southern Region 1948 - 1960.*

Right - *Pupilship Agreement between Robert Wallace Urie and Robert Steele. Robert's signature was witnessed by W P Froud, Superintendent at Portsmouth & Southsea station.'*

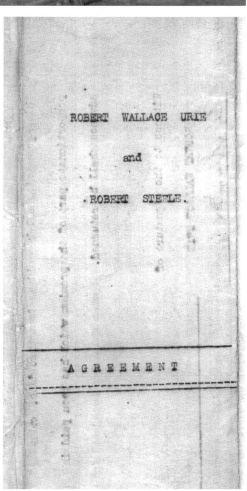

ROBERT WALLACE URIE

and

ROBERT STEELE.

A G R E E M E N T

ROY DOUGLASS STEELE

A RAILWAY CAREER 1923 - 1960

Compiled by Elizabeth Humby (née Steele)

In 2013 Noodle Books published 'Men, Machines & Maintenance at Exmouth Junction', the railway story of fitter Bob Trevelyan during the last days of steam in the shed. This prompted a letter from Mrs Elizabeth Humby who wrote with reference to her recollections of family life as the daughter of Roy Steele who had risen through the ranks of the Motive Power Department of the Southern Railway. What follows is Roy's career story, describing how life was not at all easy at the time even for a time-served and qualified engineer.

I have recently read 'MacLeod's Other Island', the story of Alistair MacLeod, the Southern Railway's first 'Assistant for the Isle of Wight'[1]. This has inspired me to write an account of my father's career on the Southern Railway, partly because I heard the name MacLeod mentioned by my parents. I also knew that my father had acted as a holiday relief in the Isle of Wight.

I was lucky enough to have (my father) Roy's papers, which did in fact show that he was asked to go to Ryde, to spend six days with Mr. J C Urie (Mr. MacLeod's predecessor) in 1928, before acting as his relief. I have not found any further reference to Roy acting as a relief, but my mother told me that he was on duty there in the mid-thirties again while Mr. MacLeod was on leave, and there may therefore have been other times.

My father was born in Southsea in 1905. Educated at Havant High School and for a short time at St. John's College, Southsea, he then spent two years at Portsmouth Municipal College, on a Mechanical Engineering course.

In 1922 my grandfather, Robert Steele of St. Martyn's Lodge, Third Avenue, Denvilles, Havant, applied for a pupilship at Eastleigh works for Roy. Roy was granted an interview with Mr. R W Urie in October that year. (Considering the impending end of the London & South Western Railway from 31 December 1922, Roy may well have been one of the last to be interviewed in LSWR days.)

For the interview at Eastleigh, Roy was accompanied by his elder brother Harold, 14 years his senior. (I believe Harold was a generous benefactor in later years so far as assisting with the considerable expenses involved in pupilship.)

The outcome of this interview was that Roy was offered a pupilship at Eastleigh commencing in January 1923, the formal agreement referring to "...Robert Wallace Urie, Locomotive Engineer, Southern Railway (South Western Section) of 56 Hill Lane, Southampton." (On other railways and at different times the term 'Premium Apprentice' was used. The meaning was the same in that the apprentice would gain experience in all the various workshops as well as the drawing office. Those who were

successful would be marked out for subsequent supervisory and management roles.)

An agreement as to the pupilage was signed between my grandfather and Mr Urie for Roy to learn the usual branches of Mechanical Engineering. The cost was £450 over three years to be paid in £150 annual instalments. The family believe my grandfather had to mortgage his house to pay for his son's fees and indeed there still was a mortgage when grandfather died suddenly in 1937, aged 74 years. One slight variation in the agreement occurred when Richard Maunsell, who had taken over from Mr Urie consequent upon the latter's retirement in 1924, wrote to Roy to continue the arrangement. Notwithstanding the cost of the pupilage, he was reimbursed the princely sum of £1 per week throughout his training.

We know only a little of Roy's life at Eastleigh, although a surviving record shows he did not necessarily spend as much time in each section as would normally be required. Partly this was due to him becoming seriously ill after contracting rheumatic fever in 1925; there is also mention of an accident of some sort. In addition to works knowledge he gained experience in the nearby running shed in both an administrative role as well as acting as a fireman. The culmination of his efforts was the gaining of Associate status with the Institute of Mechanical Engineers in 1926.

By 1927 the family had moved to 9 Knowsley Road, Cosham. Possibly Roy was already working at the nearest depot to his home, namely Fratton, for he was certainly there with the title 'Assistant to the Foreman at Fratton Locomotive Running Department[2]' in late 1928. We also know he was what was deemed 'relief staff', expected to cover any suitable short-term vacancy anywhere throughout the Southern Railway system and with the same title as he had whilst working at Fratton. (Relief staff were granted a temporary travel pass but with the strict notation that this must be returned to head office when no longer required or when expired.)

A letter in the family archive from Mr Maunsell refers to an application to the Crown Agents for Colonies in October and encloses a testimonial. He advises Roy to

Privilege Ticket Orders. For his time on the Island he was based at Ryde.

It was whilst in charge at Ryde on Sunday 9 September that an accident occurred involving one of the petrol cars. Roy completed a report dated the same day and which was sent to Surrey Warner at Eastleigh:

"Dear Sir,

I have to report that at 7.20 this morning No 2 Petrol car was proceeding trailer (No 3) first from Ryde Esplanade to the Pier Head under the control of Driver R Aylward and failed to stop correctly at the platform. In consequence the trailer collided with the stop blocks and received damage as follows:

Three lights broken
Iron hand rails and gate at leading end bent
Headstock badly fractured
Draw bar beam broken and angles bent
No damage was evident to Petrol car engine and on test brakes were found to be in good working order.
The stop blocks were driven slightly out of the vertical.

From examination of the rails, which were slightly damp outside the station, it would appear that the wheels of the

apply for another, similar, vacancy in February 1928. Subsequent to this there is no further mention of these posts nor about where they might have been.

Unfortunately, in 1928 circumstances outside Roy's control caused a temporary interruption in what might be expected to have been a gradual climb up the promotion and salary tree, for in August a letter was sent out from the General Manager's Office at Waterloo, advising staff that, *'Owing to a progressive decrease in the receipts of the railway during the current year and following the comparatively poor results of last year and the serious financial position thereby created, it has after careful consideration been decided to seek the co-operation of staff in their endeavour to overcome a difficulty which is confidently hoped and expected will prove to be of a temporary character only'.* This was a precursor to the main point, that, *'As a result of negotiations, it has been mutually agreed that the classes of staff for whom the Trade Unions act will surrender each pay day a sum equal to 2½ per cent of their gross earning''.* Continuing, *'...the Board has, therefore, decided that a similar deduction at the rate of 2½ per cent shall be made from the amount paid to the Officers, and from the earnings of all other sections of the staff not subject to National Agreements. These deductions will take effect on and after the 13 August next. The Directors have also agreed to a 2½.per cent being deducted from their fees'.*

The sombre news may have been alleviated slightly by Roy being requested to take up Mr J C Urie's duties on the Isle of Wight, prior to his Annual Leave. This was to commence on the 27 August, 1928 and was preceded by an amount of correspondence detailing his lodging allowance, pay at £260 (pro-rata) per annum whilst relieving on the Island. He was also issued with an 'All Stations' pass and arrangements were made for his signature to be accepted on

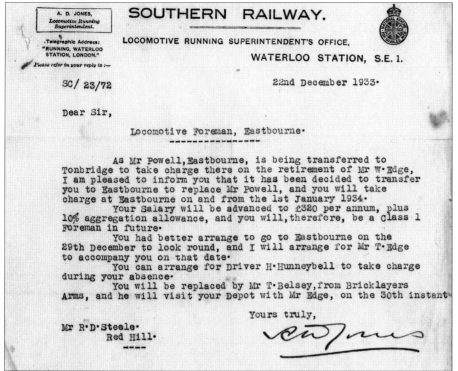

Letter reads:

A. D. JONES,
Locomotive Running
Superintendent.

·Telegraphic Address:
"RUNNING, WATERLOO
STATION, LONDON."

Please refer in your reply to :—

SOUTHERN RAILWAY.

LOCOMOTIVE RUNNING SUPERINTENDENT'S OFFICE,

WATERLOO STATION, S.E. 1.

SC/ 23/72   22nd December 1933·

Dear Sir,

Locomotive Foreman, Eastbourne·
- - - - - - - - - - - - - - - - -

As Mr Powell, Eastbourne, is being transferred to
Tonbridge to take charge there on the retirement of Mr W·Edge,
I am pleased to inform you that it has been decided to transfer
you to Eastbourne to replace Mr Powell, and you will take
charge at Eastbourne on and from the 1st January 1934·
Your Salary will be advanced to £320 per annum, plus
10% aggregation allowance, and you will,therefore, be a Class 1
Foreman in future·
You had better arrange to go to Eastbourne on the
29th December to look round, and I will arrange for Mr T·Edge
to accompany you on that date·
You can arrange for Driver H·Hunneybell to take charge
during your absence·
You will be replaced by Mr T·Belsey,from Bricklayers
Arms, and he will visit your Depot with Mr Edge, on the 30th instant·

Yours truly,

Mr R·D·Steele·
Red Hill·
- - - -

petrol car skidded approximately 24′ before coming to rest.

Two previous trips had been made with the car and trailer with a full load. On the third trip, however, eight passengers were in the trailer only, one of whom I understand received injuries to his neck from broken glass.

There was no conductor on the car at the time of the accident and after uncoupling the trailer the west side service was maintained with the petrol car unit only.

In my opinion the accident occurred through an error of judgement on the part of the driver."

Any further outcome is not reported as Roy left Ryde on 15 September. Possibly he returned to Fratton although this was not for long as on 19 October he received a letter from A D Jones, the Locomotive Running Superintendent at Waterloo to the effect that he was to be transferred to Brighton shed as Assistant Foreman in place of Mr Winchester. He was also advised that his salary would be increased to £210 pa. (We are not told what his previous salary was, although clearly when effecting temporary cover at a higher grade post – as recently on the Isle of Wight – he had been paid at the rate of the higher grade.)

Roy was also still furthering his own qualifications and gained a First Division Certificate in Railway Operating from the University of Southampton in August 1930. Shortly before this, A D Jones had also sent him details of vacancies for Junior Locomotive Engineers on the Buenos Aires and Pacific Railway Co. Ltd. in Argentina as well as another vacancy this time for a Locomotive Foreman with the Ceylon Government Railway. It is likely all men in a similar position on the SR were similarly advised although so far as Roy was concerned, no outcome is recorded[3].

Nothing is reported on Roy's time at Brighton although we do know that he unsuccessfully applied for vacancies at Reading and Gillingham. Instead his next move was in 1931 when he was appointed Assistant to Mr Sheppy, the Eastern Divisional Locomotive Superintendent, at Waterloo. A surviving letter from the time shows that Mr Sheppy had been sent a letter from Mr H Lelew, Roy's boss and Locomotive Foreman at Brighton. This stated, 'Mr. Steele has been of great assistance to me during the time I have been here, and I consider he would give satisfaction wherever he went'. Roy's next move was also his most important as he married in October 1931.

Career-wise, his experience was now put to good use as in October 1932 he was at last promoted to run his own depot, Redhill, then aged just 27. At the same time there was a further salary increase to £270 pa plus a 5% "aggregation" allowance.

A year later Roy sent a letter to head office as follows, '…although there was an increase in steam traffic at Redhill this summer, you will doubtless have noticed that the wages of this depot show a substantial decrease over the last year. Staff and engines had been reduced after electrification but electric services were unable to deal with a certain class of traffic.'

In dealing with the extra work, albeit with a reduced staff, Roy clearly felt he was being undervalued as he asks for a review of his grade to reflect his increased duties. It appears that, for the present at least, his request was ignored although an improvement came when at the end of 1933 he was advised he was to be transferred to Eastbourne with a salary increase to £320 per annum plus 10% aggregation allowance. (This equated to more than 50% increase in pay since 1928.)

A pleasing touch in connection with his move was a letter from three of the Redhill staff thanking him, '…for the perfectly fair treatment you accorded us during our term of office as Members of the L.D.C.'

Roy's tenure at Eastbourne commenced on 1 January 1934 to which end we are also now given an indication of the procedure for the transfer of management staff between depots. Accordingly on 22 December he was advised from Waterloo, "…you had better go to Eastbourne on 29 December to look around. I will arrange for Mr T Edge (who retires from 1 January 1934) to accompany you

PRIVATE.   SOUTHERN RAILWAY   AJH/SC

Reference

From LOCOMOTIVE RUNNING SUPERINTENDENT.   MY 23/72

YOUR

To   Locomotive Foreman,
        St. Leonards.

    Date   23rd May 1938.

SUBJECT:—   Transfer.

        Confirming arrangements made on the telephone on
Saturday last.

        I wish you to go to Bournemouth as from the 25th instant
for the purpose of looking round the District, and I will
leave it to you as to how long you wish to spend there.

        It will be necessary for you to finally take charge
of the Depot as from the 11th July next.

        Mr. Lane, who is succeeding you will visit St. Leonards
as from the 8th proximom for the purpose of looking round
your Depots.

        I am dealing with the question of a Pass.

                    For
                    A. Cobb

(1½)   SOUTHERN RAILWAY.   Stock 589 (10-31)

From Loco.Running Dept.   To Loco.Running Dept.
                              . St.Leonards.   My S/P
    Bournemouth Ctl.   10th.October   1938   Your

Dear Mr. Lane,

        I am sending you herewith two keys which I
omitted to hand over on leaving. One is the Safe Key and you
receive it as it was handed to me - unused. This for the simple
reason that it is of little use without a key for the outer
wooden door and the only one in existence is held by Lastes.
The other enclosure is for the "Houses of Parliament".

        Trusting all's well at your end,

                    Yours sincerely,

---

on that date. You can arrange for Driver H Hunneybell to take charge during your absence. You will be replaced at Redhill by Mr. T Belsey from Bricklayers Arms and he will visit your depot with Mr Edge on 30 inst."

From correspondence we now learn that the Southern Railway had a grading system for shed foremen, the Eastbourne role being classified as 'Class 1'. In 1935 Roy was given additional responsibility in taking charge at St Leonards. With two depots to control, there was a

further, and this time significant, salary increase to £400 pa. The family also moved to 'Fairlinks', Dorset Road, Bexhill around the same time.

The years 1937-1939 cannot have been easy for my parents. The family had grown by now with two young daughters, Eleanor and Elizabeth, although as mentioned earlier it was also in 1937 that Grandfather Steele died suddenly. As well as his railway work Roy was now also involved in sorting out his mother's financial affairs. With the house still under mortgage it was now let out, with grandmother and my Aunt Dora who had lived with her, moving to a bungalow in Portchester. My father had bought the bungalow although grandmother paid him a small rent from her pension income. Another problem at this time was the need for my sister Eleanor to receive regular 'Ultra-Violet Ray treatment' at Hastings hospital three times a week. For this purpose my mother and sister were issued with 'hospital passes' allowing reduced rate travel.

But it was not all work as my parents found time to visit the Rhine and then Bavaria for two holidays in 1936 and 1938 respectively. I recall my father commenting on the change in atmosphere within Germany during their later visit.

On 23 May 1938 Roy received a letter from Alan Cobb at Waterloo stating that he was required to go to Bournemouth two days later to 'look around the district'. The 'district' including not just the depot at Bournemouth but also Dorchester, Swanage and Hamworthy. Surprisingly Branksome is not mentioned. He would take charge at Bournemouth from 11 July with a further salary increase to £450 per annum. Roy was succeeded at St Leonards by Mr. Lane. The Bournemouth move was subsequently reported in the 'Southern Railway Magazine' in March 1939, and was the second time Roy had featured in this publication (the first was February 1938 when mention was made of his Eastbourne move). It also shows how staff moves were often reported in the magazine sometime after the actual

Armoured train at Wadebridge - see page 13. The engine is a 'conscripted' former GER 2-4-2T. It was this train that was 'lost' by the military..... .

occurrence.

Whilst at Bournemouth Roy wrote to his successor at St Leonards, Mr Lane, returning two keys which he had omitted to leave. '...one is for the safe, and you receive it as it was handed to me, 'unused': the other is for the 'Houses of Parliament'. (It appeared the safe was itself in a locked cupboard and whilst there was a key for the safe no one used it as there was no key to the cupboard!)

The reference to the prevailing atmosphere in Germany as then applied was now also being felt at home. Roy had applied for a period of leave in September 1938, his request being returned from Waterloo with the proviso, "...'on the understanding that should anything arise out of the present political situation, you must be prepared to cancel your arrangements at a moment's notice".

The following year a copy of the 'Southern Railway Magazine', dated April 1939 states that 'The annual dinner of Bournemouth locomotive staff was held at the Gervis Hall Restaurant recently, under the chairmanship of Mr R Steele, Locomotive Foreman. In proposing the toast of 'The Southern Railway', he referred to the 'square deal', various developments in electrification, and the building of new locomotives. He commented that already three new goods engines had been allocated to their depot and a number of new type locomotives designed for express work were under construction[4]. When during the course of the evening, Roy made reference to the 'Schools' class engines,

S C Townroe, who was in charge of Dorchester depot, presented Roy with the scholastic mortar-board cap, causing much laughter. S C Townroe commented in much later years that he thought Roy's time in Bournemouth was his happiest.

In September 1939, my brother Howard was born, the same month of course that war broke out. Despite his spell at Bournemouth recalled as being happy, Roy's main interest was in 'the locomotive' itself whilst he was keen to further his experience and his career. He was desirous of upgrading his professional status to that of AIMechE and consequently applied for what we may assume was a workshop post as his application was addressed both to Mr. A Cobb and also to O V S Bulleid at Deepdene. (We are not told what this post was.) He supported his application with the comment that the Institute did not consider his present status entitled him to full membership.

A reply was received from Cobb expressing some sympathy with his situation, although nothing further occurred as he was still at Bournemouth in June 1940. Instead he was advised he would have a further increase in salary to £468 which included a 'War Advance' of £18. Another increase of £25 was awarded in January 1941.

A rather different letter was written by my father in September 1940, to the Loco. Running Supt., Eastleigh. In this he wishes to purchase 18lbs. of fractured 'Bogie Control Spring Bolts, etc'. and 1 cwt. of defective timber

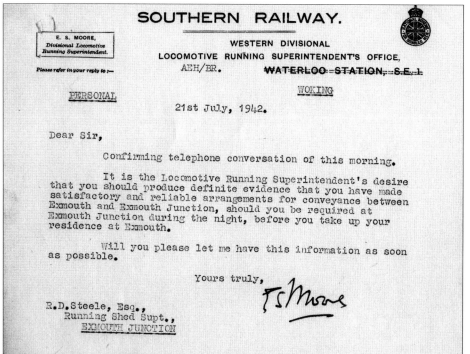

SOUTHERN RAILWAY.

Orphanage, Woking (Western Division) from August 1942.

Meanwhile, my father had to negotiate lodging allowances in Exeter, not an easy task for as he states, '…25,000 persons from the area were rendered homeless during the Blitz and the chances of an outsider obtaining accommodation under such circumstances require no reiteration on my part.' Eventually accommodation was found but there then followed a further battle for a removal allowance – finally agreed at £19 14s, with an additional fight for the expense of making the house habitable.

The house we had was at 44 Feltrim Avenue, Exeter. When my mother first visited it was roofless, having been blown off in the blitz. The local authority restored the roof and ceilings but the landlord refused to repair a damaged wall as he feared prejudicing War Damage Compensation. In the end my father had to attend to the worst eyesores himself as well as providing blackout curtains, lino, etc. In addition our furniture was considerably damaged by Pickfords during the move, something my father commented upon that he had never experienced in five previous moves.

consisting of 'shelves and partitions etc. from breakdown vans now broken up, as scrap'. He was prepared to offer 1/- for the metal and 1/- for the firewood. It is believed it was a successful bid, with the material likely to have been intended for an Air Raid Shelter he built on to our home in Pine Avenue to replace one in the garden, the latter probably of the 'Anderson' type.

A further move took place in May 1942 when Roy was transferred to Exmouth Junction as Running Shed Superintendent. He immediately requested the necessary 'Southern and Great Western passes', both to cover his own district and those lines owned by the GWR upon which he might have to travel.

Exeter was of course bombed during WW2, particularly on the night of 4 May 1942. Roy described to family members how he had arrived in Exeter the morning after its biggest raid with the streets deserted and how eerie it all seemed. Roy was in lodgings at Exeter but returned home to Bournemouth for occasional week-end leave. His Exmouth Junction posting brought with it a substantial pay increase to £528 per annum, the amount involved reflecting the importance of the post.

With damage to housing in the area, accommodation was obviously difficult and despite finding a suitable house in Exmouth, objections were made to his living there as this was considered to be too far from Exmouth Junction should he be required at night. At Exmouth Junction he combined his role with that of Chief Air Raid Warden: he was also responsible for taking charge in the event of any serious derailment. (His tin helmet and stirrup pump were still hanging up in the garage years later.)

One role he was delighted to accept was that of Joint President of the Southern Railway Servants

We moved in on 29 August, 1942. Chickens brought from Bournemouth were re-housed for eggs for the children and 'Shell Egg Coupons' were surrendered. (The chickens escaped once and flew into the pine trees at the bottom of the garden.) We children had gas-masks, my brother's being the Mickey Mouse type. My sister and I were sent to the local convent school, close enough to walk to and home again for lunch. I was never happy there but my sister liked it well enough and I believe the teaching standard was probably excellent. The school had a large Morrison shelter in the hall, but I can only remember having to use it a couple of times.

As our house was some distance from the depot (but also the only property available), my father had to apply for a telephone allowance, this being stipulated as. '… to be used for work purposes and then only in emergencies'. Meanwhile his persistence paid off as he was granted a further £15-12s.-6d in December for house expenses.

In September 1942, Roy had received what would normally have been his call-up papers but in October was told, 'Deferment has been asked for in your case'. However, in March 1943 a further communication required him to register at the local office of the Ministry of Labour. The Southern Railway regarded him as an 'Essential Worker' and consequently he was advised to describe himself as

ROY DOUGLASS STEELE   A RAILWAY CAREER 1923 -1960

follows, "Maintenance and Repair of Southern Railway Locomotives. Management of Locomotive Depots and of Enginemen and Mechanical Staff. Responsible for all matters pertaining to; the supply of Motive Power in my area and for Breakdown Work (clearing the line in the event of mishap or Enemy Action). Regarded as 'Key Official' by Southern Railway Company".

Whilst we know his appointment had been to Exmouth Junction itself, a later entry in the 'Southern Magazine' refers to his area as covering not just the depot but also the Western District: an area from Lyme Regis and Seaton in the east to Callington and Padstow in the west.

Previous deferment from service in the Armed Forces did not exclude Roy from a later interview in Plymouth where it was made it clear that this was for the purpose of assessing his general capabilities and suitability for inclusion in a pool of names of persons considered suitable for commissioned rank should the need for technical personnel become pressing in the future. He then had to attend a medical examination and was placed in Grade II, being informed he would be included in the Register of men qualified to receive Commissions in the technical branches of the Armed Forces. 'The fact that your name has been entered on this register does not mean that you will necessarily be among those finally selected for service in the Armed Forces either in the near future or at any time'. In the event he would remain with the Southern Railway.

One amusing incident from this time may be recounted. An 'armoured train' was operated by the Southern Railway and was based at Wadebridge. In reality this was probably little more than as a reassurance to the local populace but hauled by a similarly armoured engine, it was run around certain of the North Cornwall / Devon lines during night time, returning to its siding in the early hours. In charge was a young Lieutenant. Unfortunately one day the local pick-up goods needed to access a wagon or two that had been stabled behind the train. Rather than shunt the military vehicles out of the way, the guard attached the lot. The consternation of the military that evening is best imagined when they arrived to find their train disappeared. (It was eventually located having been berthed in a siding at the next station down the line.)

In April 1943 Roy's salary was increased with a 'War Advance' of £53 6s. per annum, giving a total of £578 6s. per annum.

In November of the same year letters passed between my father, Deepdene and the Inspector of Taxes, regarding clothing allowances. Supervising Staff were normally supplied with overcoat, mackintosh and leggings, plus a special suit of overalls because of the need to deal with the 'Merchant Navy' class engines. My father states that on top of personal inspection of locomotive details, coaling plants, footplate work and attendance at derailments etc., he has to make 'a reasonably presentable appearance', owing to frequent inter-departmental meetings and public contacts with subsequent need for dry-cleaning of clothing. He adds that the company had never supplied him with overalls during his railway career.

There was also a query over his claim for a cycle allowance. This was answered by my father as follows, '… my house is three miles from the depot and as there is no bus service after 9.00pm and none at all on Sunday mornings, a cycle is essential.'

Another move for our family occurred in 1945, when a letter from Deepdene in April confirmed Roy's promotion to Assistant Western Divisional Superintendent of Motive Power at Woking. With it came a salary increase to £600 per annum backdated to March of that year. His new boss would be Mr. E S Moore who my father had

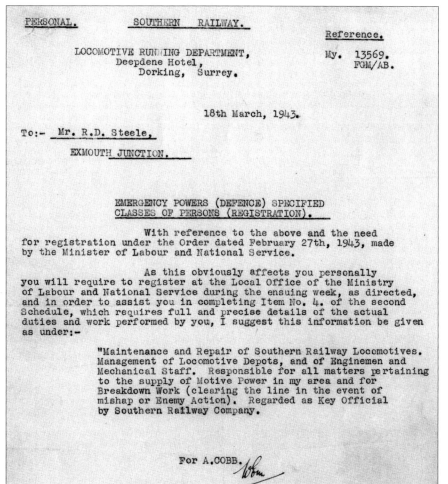

No 21C4 'Cunard White Star' after arriving at Exmouth Junction on 18 November 1942 having been shot-up whilst hauling a train near Whimple. (See also 'Southern Way Special No 5: Wartime Southern Part 2'.)

Jeremy Cobb collection

received letters from since 1928, and who he must have met and known quite well.

Upon leaving Exeter, Roy received a letter from the Exmouth Junction Local Departmental Committee, 'to thank you for the courteous manner in which you have at all times received us, and for the friendly atmosphere that prevailed in all our discussions. Our best wishes are extended to you in the new sphere of work to which you are now going'.

A further letter came from the Mr W H Shortt, Divisional Engineer, Central Station, Exeter, who states, 'I am sorry to see from the *Railway Gazette* that the West of England is losing you but send my congratulations and best wishes for the new job.' Another letter came from the St. John's Ambulance Welfare Officer and Centre Secretary, stating that at a recent meeting of the District Committee for the Western Division, a unanimous vote had been passed to the effect that I should ask you to accept an expression of thanks on their behalf for the interest and support given by you at all times.

I think the whole family must have been sad to leave Exeter behind. Our house had a public footpath to the River Exe running behind it, which we could use to get to Exeter. There was also the excitement of a weir and a paper mill on the way. Further along were some large warehouses that featured much later in the TV series 'The Onedin Line', but at the time we passed had large piles of cows' horns outside. We walked that way to reach St. Thomas's Station for trips to Dawlish Warren, which we all seemed to enjoy, perhaps the highlight being when an American 'Duck' (DUKW) took us children for rides across the sands and through shallow water. This was towards the end of the war and I am sure this fostered good relations with the local population. We also had our one and only trip on the footplate of railway engine one Sunday morning, when our father took us into Exeter for a ride on a 'shunter'.

We had half-a-dozen other children to play within our cul-de-sac and used a cleaned up bomb site and woods for our games. Best of all we had mother's Aunt Sophie living in a flat on St. David's Hill in Exeter.

The War was now over and the move to Woking in 1945 raised the problem of housing for the Steele family as we had previously always lived in rented property

There was a suggestion that my father should be accommodated in part of Station House at Walton-on-Thames, but then it was decided to award this to the incumbent Station Master Mr Mould, who required three bedrooms. What remained of the property would just not be large enough for our family.

In the end Roy took the plunge into home ownership and in July my father paid the deposit on our new home - which my mother had chosen. It was renamed 'Polzeath', after happy Cornish holidays. Located in Horsell Birch opposite the Common, it was to be our home for the next 17 years. The mortgage of £1,800 was advanced by the Southern Railway and the remainder of the expenses, £179, were settled by my father with some difficulty. The purchase was finalised in October 1945 although in the meanwhile my sister had already started attending the Grammar School for Girls in Woking. My brother and I were enrolled at Horsell C of E school, which was much more child friendly after the Convent.

In January 1947, Roy was appointed for what was to be a short spell as assistant to T E Chrimes, Motive Power Superintendent at Waterloo. Again the move, which was of course a promotion, came with an increased salary of £773 per annum, once more backdated to January.

After just nine months he made the move back to Woking, this time in the top job there as Western Divisional Motive Power Superintendent. He had also now reached the dizzy heights of £1,000 pa. It was at this point that he wrote to R M T Richards, Traffic Manager, Waterloo in September, ' to express my deep appreciation of the confidence you have placed in me deciding on my new appointment'. A later note shows that E S Moore had retired in 1947, so this new appointment was my father replacing his old boss.

The family had known Mr Moore quite well. He lived in a lovely house by the river at Weybridge and owned a fleet of small boats which we were invited to sample on family visits. I recall he took us out in a skiff or a rowing boat and also owned a single sculler and a canoe.

Another wartime incident, this time at Halwill Junction in 1944. (See 'Southern Way Special No 8: The other side of the Southern'.)
Jeremy Cobb collection

PS (3/7)   *Supt. of Motive Power.*

SOUTHERN RAILWAY

GENERAL MANAGER'S OFFICE,
WATERLOO STATION, S.E. 1.

CIRCULAR No. 279.   *27th March*, 1947.

TO ALL CONCERNED

STAFF CHANGES.

The following have effect from the dates shown :—

TRAFFIC DEPARTMENT

Effective 1st January, 1947.

MR. R. D. STEELE, appointed Assistant to Superintendent of Motive Power.

MR. J. WATSON, appointed Assistant Divisional Superintendent of Motive Power, Western Division.

MR. F. L. HOWARD, appointed Assistant Divisional Superintendent of Motive Power, Eastern Division.

Effective 1st May, 1947.

MR. F. H. MARSHALL, appointed London District Freight Superintendent, vice MR. E. E. YOUNG, who retires.

CHIEF CIVIL ENGINEER'S DEPARTMENT.

Effective 1st February, 1947.

MR. R. COGGER, appointed Assistant to Signal Engineer.

E. J. MISSENDEN,
General Manager.

No 34006 'Bude' at Marylebone in 1948 having arrived with the 8.25 am from Manchester. This was a test run prior to the full interchange trials. Roy Steele is stood by the engine.
A Earle-Edwards

The Nationalisation of the railways in 1948 was to bring great changes and a letter from Mr Chrimes at Waterloo Station, dated 14 October 1948, asked staff on salaries over £630 per annum who desired to be considered for promotion and be prepared to move anywhere on British Railways, to give brief particulars of experience and nature of post to which promotion is desired. Roy replied that he was prepared to consider promotion anywhere on the British Railways He gave details of his experience from 1921 to 1947 and the nature of the post which he would seek, namely 'Chief Officer'.

The years 1947-1948 and his new role resulted in less hands-on work and more administration. Even so he was responsible for providing the motive power for some high profile duties including Royal Trains. One such occasion was when the whole family was invited to witness the departure of the then Princess Elizabeth and Prince Philip from Waterloo en route to their honeymoon destination at Romsey. He also provided locomotives for the films 'Anna Karenina' in 1947 and 'The Red Shoes' in 1948.

In March 1950 Mr Hopkins, the Chief Regional Officer, Waterloo, informed Roy of a new post as District Motive Power Superintendent, Nine Elms at a salary of £1,200 per annum, to take effect from 27 February, 1950. Mr.Hopkins added his congratulations and best wishes. My father wrote and thanked him stating, 'I assure you that the efforts that were made to secure the continued success of the Western Division will in no way be lessened with the new organisation and its Electrical associations under British Railways'.

Correspondence shows that despite his 'District role' he continued to be based at Woking, covering Nine Elms from there. His leave entitlement was increased to four weeks per annum in 1950 and his salary to £1,275 in 1951, at which time he received the following in a letter from Mr. Chrimes. 'I would like to say how pleased I am that this merit award has been granted in your favour and to take this opportunity of expressing thanks for the good work you have put into your District since reorganization took effect'. A further increase of salary in 1951 and another in 1952 took the amount to £1,470 per annum.

My father was still paying for a mortgage on our house in Horsell near Woking at this time and was informed in February 1953 that the interest was £45. He was also informed that the maximum he could receive in salary was £1,550 per annum, increases awarded solely on merit. He received this maximum in January 1954 and was again thanked by Mr Chrimes for, '...the work you have put into your District under difficult circumstances.'

We are not told what these circumstances were but they may well have been personal. Father had developed symptoms of MS and had been admitted to The National Hospital in London for assessment during 1952-1954. He still carried on working but there was at least one period in 1956 when he was confined to bed. In 1959 a letter from the Ministry of Pensions and National Insurance referred to a

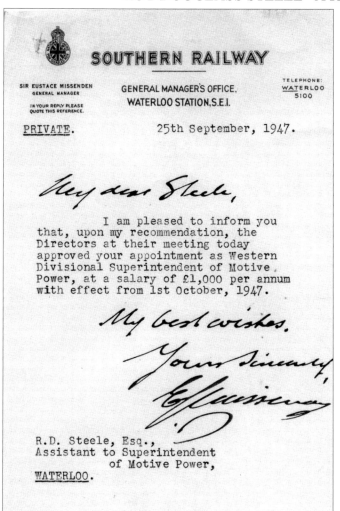

SOUTHERN RAILWAY

SIR EUSTACE MISSENDEN
GENERAL MANAGER

GENERAL MANAGER'S OFFICE,
WATERLOO STATION, S.E.I.

TELEPHONE:
WATERLOO
5100

IN YOUR REPLY PLEASE
QUOTE THIS REFERENCE.

PRIVATE.   25th September, 1947.

My dear Steele,

I am pleased to inform you that, upon my recommendation, the Directors at their meeting today approved your appointment as Western Divisional Superintendent of Motive Power, at a salary of £1,000 per annum with effect from 1st October, 1947.

My best wishes.

Yours sincerely,

R.D. Steele, Esq.,
Assistant to Superintendent
        of Motive Power,
WATERLOO.

SOUTHERN RAILWAY

GENERAL MANAGER'S OFFICE,
WATERLOO STATION, S.E. 1.

CIRCULAR No. 282.   25th September, 1947.

TO ALL CONCERNED.

STAFF CHANGES.

The following have effect from the dates shown :—

TRAFFIC DEPARTMENT.
Effective 1st July, 1947.

MR. A. E. HOARE, to Assistant Superintendent of Motive Power.

MR. G. L. NICHOLSON, to Assistant to Superintendent of Motive Power.

Effective 1st October, 1947.

MR. E. S. MOORE, Western Divisional Superintendent of Motive Power, to retire.

MR. R. D. STEELE, to Western Divisional Superintendent of Motive Power.

MR. J. RODGERS, to Assistant to Superintendent of Motive Power.

MR. W. H. SCUTT, to Senior Assistant Divisional Superintendent, London West Division.

MR. H. E. BARBER, to Assistant Divisional Superintendent, London East Division.

MR. W. H. WOOD, to Assistant Divisional Superintendent, Southern Division.

E. J. MISSENDEN,

---

payment for incapacity benefit. During the last year or two he was working he would use the small windowless Paymaster's office on Woking Station as this was more convenient for him. At this time he was involved more as a Civil Engineer, examining Victorian documents on tunnels, all presented 'in spidery writing'.

Roy retired on health grounds in 1960 and was awarded a lump sum of £1,643 and a pension of £800 pa for life.

Letters to my father at this time conveyed many kind messages. One in particular came from P A White, the Assistant General Manager (Traffic) who stated, 'In thanking you very warmly and sincerely for all your efforts since you commenced railway service over 37 years ago, I am indeed mindful of all you have done towards maintaining the high standard of achievement for the Region generally and the motive power in particular. That your most valuable attributes will no longer available to the Region over the difficult years ahead is regrettable in the extreme'. The letter ends, 'Kindest regards and best wishes' to both my father and my mother.

Stephen Townroe, Roy's contemporary, later wrote to the family and remarked that my father would not have got much pleasure out of the deterioration of steam after he retired, broken-down engines driven by men without the pride drivers took in pre -1939 days. He added he was glad to have known my father, who was also a confidant of his, 'full of commonsense advice'. In the normal course of events Roy would have reached retirement about the same time as the 'King Arthur', 'Lord Nelson' and 'Schools' classes were going to the scrap heap. Townroe adds, 'By then nobody at Marylebone had any time for steam, or officers brought up in steam'.

Suffering from deteriorating health, the house and garden at Horsell were now unsuitable for Roy as he was confined to a wheel-chair and my mother looked for a suitable property in Lee-on-the-Solent in Hampshire. She chose a bungalow that was easily adapted and much nearer my sister and her family in Winchester as well as other family members in Bedhampton. I changed my job to offices in Southsea and we moved to Lee in the summer of 1962. My parents enjoyed living by the sea again and I had a lovely wedding there in 1963. Our son was born in 1965 and so my father was able to see him for a short while before his death in 1968. Family tradition also continues for my son went on to become a full-time member of staff on

Roy with the badge of office 'bowler-hat' on the footplate of No 647 at Brighton Works, c1930.

the Mid-Hants Railway some years later, helping to restore the classes of locomotives my father had worked with, including Bulleid locos which gave Roy so much trouble.

In the preparation of these notes some extra items were found which, whilst not fitting neatly anywhere within the previous text, are worthy of inclusion. It was clear my father had a special regard for the 'King Arthur' design for during his working life he spent any spare time he had, building a 3½" gauge model of *Sir Bors de Gani*s. Complete in every detail, it was only ever steamed once, at the Guildford Model Engineering Exhibition in the 1950s. It also had a mention in the *Southern Railway Magazine* during 1939. At one time it was also exhibited on the Isle of Wight where it aroused a 'great deal of interest'. It was finally painted by a member of the Portsmouth Model Engineering Society, who gave the model a home before it was returned to the family some years later. It remains in the family.

As his daughter I have a strong memory of a 'Merchant Navy' locomotive pulling into Woking station in the mid-1940s, when my father introduced us to the engine type that had given him so much trouble.

The class appeared in 1941 and was followed by the similar but slightly smaller 'West Country' class in 1945. Bulleid's predecessor had been R.E L Maunsell who had followed in the tradition established by Robert Urie of 'Make everything get-at-able'. Bulleid had no time for the 'King Arthurs', but was delighted with the 'Schools'. (My father had worked with them at St. Leonards in the mid-1930s, when he had an early batch of the class and kept a strict eye on their behaviour. He also mentioned them in a speech at Bournemouth in 1939.)

My cousin says that, in conversations with my father, he was told that the valve gear on the 'Merchant Navy' class very soon began to give problems, to the extent that my father had to take them out of service at Exmouth Junction. This didn't please Mr Bulleid who would emerge from his office on Waterloo Station expecting to see his new engine on the front of an incoming express from the West of England. He would get on the phone to my father

demanding to know why his engine had been 'stopped'. My father had to tell him that the valve gear was giving problems and they didn't yet know what to do about it. They had not been given any specific instructions or information and so had to take a set of valve gear to pieces to find out how it worked. My father did concede that when these engines were rebuilt in 1956 with conventional Walschaert's valve gear, they were very successful.

As a comparison, during WW2 the American locomotives that were shipped to this country, according to father, came with an impressive instruction book and all the tools required.

I don't remember my father talking about particular engines, but I do recall him reacting with wry amusement when the 'King Arthur' class was being withdrawn from service and an attempt was made at Longmoor Army Camp to blow one up. It transpired that *Merlin* could only be compelled to jump the rails.

My father also recalled an incident when a large railway gun was transported to the West Country for calibration. Signals and other overhead obstructions had to be removed or adjusted for clearance for the gun's journey. All these gantries etc. then had to be restored, probably after only a few shots had been fired and the gun returned to the South East coast. According to supplemental notes provided by Gordon William (Bill) Batten, Okehampton station was used by the Army, being the nearest point to Dartmoor Camp for weapon training and manoeuvres. This may well have been the destination of the gun referred to. Bill Batton also comments on 'Newcourt' depot, which was used by American Forces. This was located on the Exmouth branch and was provided with rail access, trains being worked by SR locomotives from Exmouth Junction yard as necessary. The items and vehicles moved to Newcourt included a mix of box and open wagons, jeeps, motor-cycles, anti-aircraft guns and general stores. Also hauled were locomotives of the S160 type, the tenders of which were loaded with tool kits and spares to keep them going once in service. ('Bill' Batton had been employed at Exmouth Junction by Roy Steele on 16 July 1942 resulting in a career that lasted for 50 years.)

1 – Holne Publishing, by Terry Hastings and Roger Silsbury.

2- The term 'Foreman' as applicable to a running shed was the equivalent of what was in later years the Shedmaster.

3 – As an aside it may be interesting to relate the conditions of service that went with the Ceylon appointment, this indicated a salary of £400 rising to £525 by annual increments. The vacancy was based on a three year posting and included either free accommodation or rent allowance. There was also free travel from England for the successful applicant, his wife and up to four children (all travelling second class) at commencement and end of the engagement.

4 – This must be one of the first references to the intentions of Mr Bulleid that would culminate in the 'Merchant Navy' class in 1941.

FAWLEY FOCUS

Authorised as far back as 1903, the branch line to Fawley on the west side of Southampton water was not opened to passengers until 20 July 1925 and even then it was built as a Light Railway under the terms of the 1896 Act. Local patronage was never particularly heavy, yet the line continued in operation running its quiet way through two intermediate stations at Marchwood and Hythe until closed to passengers in 1966. In its final years passenger workings were in the hands of 'Hampshire DEMUs', a shuttle service operating usually between Fawley and Southampton Central.

The route still survives as a goods line in 2014, indeed it has now been bereft of passenger trains for longer than they were in operation. There are two reasons for its retention, the first a private siding at Marchwood leading to the Marchwood Military Port, and secondly the existence and subsequent expansion of the petroleum-based products transported by rail from Fawley refinery. Up to the early 1970s this had included aviation fuel but the presence of an underground pipeline has ended this particular traffic although LPG and other oil-based derivatives still account for movements from the terminus.

Notwithstanding substantial housing development, particularly as far south as Hythe, calls to reinstate a passenger service have not met with any success, the latest attempt being vetoed in January 2014. As a means of lessening road congestion in the area it is to be hoped reinstatement will be considered again, the powers-that-be seeking reasons to open the railway rather than seeming to look for reasons not to do so. A full passenger resumption from Fawley is unlikely to happen, not least because the station area has now been incorporated within the security compound surrounding the actual refinery.

Partly because of its obscure location and limited traffic, the railway has never been the most recorded, but this recently discovered collection provide for a rare glimpse at the infrastructure at Fawley (including overleaf the seldom recorded goods shed). Architecture-wise it could never be said Fawley (and the other similarly designed stations on the line) was particularly attractive, but they were at least functional. The basic facilities will be noted, but then so will the lack of any passengers, something which of course contributed to passenger closure.

Building detail at Fawley. The goods shed here was unique on the line yet arrived second-hand from one of the stations on the Meon Valley route south from Alton, probably around the time the Fawley line opened. What is not certain is where the shed had originated. Its twins remained at Farringdon and Wickham well into the 1970s, whilst that at West Meon is believed to have remained on its original site post-1925. That leaves the origins as having either been from East Tisted, Privett or even Droxford. At this stage it is tempting to suggest Privett as the most likely location, for it was here in 1922 that economy was made with the closure of the passing loop. So if that occurred in 1922 might other economy have similarly taken place at that time meaning the shed was removed on that date? It seems unlikely an unwanted / under used asset would remain standing. Similar pros and cons can be addressed reference East Tisted, the company minutes books making no reference to the move. Paul Hersey collection.

THE CHESSINGTON BRANCH UNDER CONSTRUCTION

Photographs by Frank Foote, notes by Mike King

(Just as we were going to press with issue No 26, Mike King turned up the following views….)

Frank Foote made a number of visits to the line during the spring of 1938, just before opening to Tolworth on 29 May, recording construction work in progress on the extension to Chessington South, opened a year later on 28 May 1939. The writer spent his childhood in Chessington and was a regular commuter from Chessington North between 1970 and 1976.

One of the main engineering features was the three-span bridge over the Hogsmill River, between Malden Manor and Tolworth stations . This was 140 ft long and constructed like all the other bridges on the line using steel girders encased in concrete. The structure looks fine when pictured in late April 1938 but the effects of the elements and corrosion have done nothing to enhance the appearance. The river (here little wider than a stream) actually flows through the centre span while footpaths occupy each side span. The watercourse may have been diverted during construction but had been returned to the natural alignment some time before the picture was taken. The embankments were put up after the bridge was completed – being a mixture of the local clay soil and hardcore from London slum clearance – the local clay being notoriously unstable on its own. Apart from near Motspur Park Junction and at Chessington South most of the line ran on high embankments. There is evidence of chain-link fencing on concrete posts – these being standard components manufactured at Exmouth Junction concrete works. The whole looks very stark and functional but wholly in keeping with the 1930s' art deco movement. The wires crossing the picture are high-tension power lines running parallel at this point and are nothing to do with the railway.

THE CHESSINGTON BRANCH UNDER CONSTRUCTION

Right - A view looking south along Bridge Road, Chessington, with the Blackamoor's Head public house and Moor Lane School buildings visible in the distance . The concrete bridge abutments are complete – just seen behind the contractor's (Edmund Nuttall & Sons) temporary trestle bridge over the road. This carries a line of narrow gauge rails (seen in later pictures) and was the only road to be crossed other than on the level, as we shall see. One bridge girder is in position beyond the sheer legs and crane, while there is another derrick crane on the far side of the bridge . Were these sufficient to lift the girder into place or was it jacked up from street level? Not a hard hat or item of protective clothing is visible and the road appears to be closed off with nothing more sophisticated than a plank of wood placed across it!! The site of Chessington North station is to the left, the station forecourt would eventually occupy the land through the bridge on the left hand side of the road. Piles of roofing tiles in the foreground are for housing developments going on behind the photographer. At this date (late April 1938) the suburban housing boom was hitting Chessington big time, thanks to the recent opening of the A3 Kingston by-pass.

Bottom - Frank has now moved under the sheer legs seen in the previous picture and this view is towards the contractor's compound and site office – situated in what would become the forecourt of Chessington North station. The first bridge girder is now seen in close-up; this being on the south (down) side of the bridge. The girder proclaims that it was assembled by The Teesside Bridge Engineering Company of Middlesbrough and the question remains – how was it transported to site? At this time the nearest operational stations were Tolworth (just), Surbiton and Ewell West but all were several miles distant by road while the nearest river access was probably Kingston. Each end of the girder was labelled up, so that the gang on site knew which way round to position it, while the weight (58 tons) was also painted on. Did another larger crane arrive with the load in order to lift it into place?

Above - *Taken about a month later – certainly some time during May 1938 – and from the same location as the last picture. The up side girder is now in position and the decking spans are being assembled on the roadway (again note the plank across!) while some are already in place. All of these would soon be encased in concrete so the final appearance will be as the Hogsmill river bridge. This was done to try to reduce ongoing maintenance (steel needs regular painting – concrete would not) but unfortunately this allowed the steel to rust unseen inside its concrete cocoon. Note the lack of any nearby habitation - this would soon change and North Parade shopping centre now occupies the site where the trees stand, while housing now fills every available space. It was only World War 2 and the instigation of Green Belt planning restrictions that stopped this happening all the way to Leatherhead.*

Opposite top - *Our final picture at Bridge Road (was this new as well – the name could hardly be more appropriate – or was it renamed to coincide with the railway's arrival?), taken on 29th May 1938 – opening day at Tolworth. We now view the bridge from the Chessington South end beyond the concrete abutment wall, looking towards Chessington North station, which may be seen rising between the left-hand bridge girder and the narrow gauge railway bridge. Most (perhaps all?) of the decking girders are now in place and encasement in concrete will soon commence. Infilling of the embankment towards Chessington South has now started. Notice the continuous checkrails on the narrow gauge bridge and the less than perfect alignment. The contract was shared between Edmund Nuttall and Sir Robert McAlpine but the exact demarcation is unclear. Did McAlpine's build the section from Motspur Park Junction to Tolworth with Nuttall continuing to Chessington South or was the division by civil engineering, earthworks and railway installation? Both firms were well qualified to carry out all disciplines. The writer ought to know – he served his first five career years as a site engineer with McAlpine's and the concrete work is undoubtedly characteristic of "Concrete Bob" McAlpine.*

Opposite bottom - *This is Moor Lane bridge, just east of Chessington North station almost complete save for finishing of the corner pilasters. The view is taken looking north towards the writer's childhood home and the surroundings now look very different since the early 1950s with housing in all directions. The steelwork is now fully encased and there is a concrete mixer visible to the right, with a winch to enable a bucket to be raised to the top of the pier – still enshrouded in timber formwork. The narrow gauge railway crosses the road on the level between the bridge and the fences visible behind. Apart from a few notices and a rope strung between metal stakes, there is little to prevent the public from entering the site (it clearly did not stop Frank but we can only assume he asked permission first!).*

Opposite top - *Moor Lane bridge again, but now looking at 90 degrees to the last picture towards Tolworth. Frank is now standing approximately on the site of the up platform at Chessington North station (albeit about 30 feet lower down!). We can see the winch on the far right pilaster and formwork around two of the others. Little or no embankment fill has yet been placed on this side of the abutment. Bridge Road bridge (in a far less advanced state of construction) is behind the photographer. The area of fields and trees to the right are now all occupied by housing development. Date is again May 1938.*

Opposite bottom *- Frank has now walked through the construction site for half a mile or so towards Tolworth and in the distance we are looking at the completed Cox Lane bridge abutment wall just right of centre with the start of Oakcroft Road trading estate factories, served from the Kingston by-pass, to the left, partly obscured by the trees. Nearer we have the "privy", complete with pole – supporting what might be a simple signal for the narrow gauge railway perhaps – or maybe you just hoisted a flag if in occupation!! Anyway, moving on…… The narrow gauge railway system was quite extensive and we even have a passing loop while Cox Lane is crossed twice on the level, either side of the new bridge. In those days the road led nowhere – very different to today where it accesses the Chessington light industrial estate and leads through to Tolworth via Jubilee Way.*

Above - *Moving on to Tolworth, this picture was taken on the same day as the Hogsmill River bridge, in April 1938. The view is behind the down station platform and is looking east across the Kingston Road (now A240), whose double-span bridge may be seen. The rail-built up starting signal (on the London end of the down platform) is in place and the construction of the platform back wall is proceeding using Exmouth Junction pre-cast concrete fence panels. There was a substantial drop down to road level at this point. Construction of the down side waiting room is in progress, using common bricks which will be faced with concrete (the Chessington stations used facing bricks and less concrete cladding) and the concrete staircase up from subway level may be seen just beyond it. All four stations were at a very different height to street level (three above and Chessington South below) and three flights of stairs were needed between the two levels. These kept late-arriving commuters fit if they were not to miss the train – take it from me!! Three of the goods yard sidings are laid, with buffer stops on the right-hand pair but nothing as yet on the left-hand one. There is a rail-mounted cement mixer on this track, supplying the bricklayers with mortar. The "Chisarc" roof to the down platform canopy is just seen at left, along with the Crittall metal window frames – another good source of rust if not regularly repainted.*

Opposite top - *We are now on the down platform at Tolworth, looking towards London, on Sunday 29th May 1938 – opening day – not that there appears to be much custom or interest. The rather heavy "Chisarc" canopies are most apparent (those at the two Chessington stations were lighter, leading to the possible explanation that this part of the line was built by the other contractor – or maybe the design was refined somewhat?). Nevertheless, the appearance is clean and modern; but today, time and exposure, plus the graffiti merchants, have done their worst. The new signal box is on the right – flat-roofed and concrete faced again but using a 20-lever frame recovered from elsewhere and still without its name board. At this time and for exactly 12 months this was the terminus – electric trains reversing in the down platform and gaining the up line via a trailing crossover beyond the Kingston Road overbridge. Clearly the up line platform track has yet to be fully fettled. At this time the trains failed to match the futuristic look of the stations – mostly being pre-Grouping wooden-bodied vehicles on newer underframes and new modern stock would not become commonplace until 1946 onwards. Despite this, some of the older stock would continue to be seen right up until 1960.*

Opposite bottom - *Turning through 180 degrees we see the line continuing towards Chessington; Oakcroft Road factories are just visible in front of the trees while the houses to the right are on the new A3 Kingston by-pass. The ringed signal arm tells the driver he is leaving a signalled area and entering the contractor's worksite. On the left are the sidings of Tolworth yard, with nine various railway open wagons (from all the Big Four companies) plus two Stephenson Clarke coal wagons at the far end – probably locomotive coal for the contractor. Further along the up line is a train of wagons topped and tailed by a brake van, while contractor's locomotives and a crane occupy the down line and the yard headshunt in the distance. By the 1960s a modern domestic coal concentration depot was built in the yard where the wagons stand, complete with coal pens and rotating conveyor belt to transfer the various grades of coal from hopper wagon to pen. A Drewry 204hp shunter (later class 04) was permanently allocated to the yard for shunting purposes from 1969 until 1994 – number remembered as D2310 but it was later joined by sister engine D2246.*

Above - *Frank has now walked (or cycled by the look of it?) beyond Tolworth goods yard and is now standing in King George V playing fields, looking towards the Kingston by-pass – just visible through the pedestrian occupation bridge. This was built just like all the others on the line, despite having a span of little more than 12 feet and at this point goes under three tracks – up and down running lines plus yard headshunt. Above stand two contractor's 0-6-0 saddle tank locomotives – the left hand one is named 'Ashendon'*, that on the right cannot be read. These are probably owned by Sir Robert McAlpine, so are likely to have been painted green (most things McAlpine were!). They had a preference for the products of Hudswell Clarke and at least one of the locos is of this parentage (further information would be most welcome). To the right is a steam crane (probably also McAlpine's – they had a yard at Hayes in West London where most of their equipment was based) while an ex-Midland Railway 3-plank dropside in bauxite livery stands beyond.*

* see over.   31

For our final picture Frank has walked a few hundred yards further towards Chessington and taken this view looking back towards Tolworth. In the distance the steam crane and the two locomotives seen in the last picture are visible, while on the bridge yet another contractor's locomotive is parked. The bridge gives vehicular access to King George's playing fields pavilion and the timber hut occupies the site of the present headshunt siding buffers, explaining the wide bridge abutment on that side. The temporary tank on a timber trestle base provides water for the locos, with a timber stockade for coal alongside. Below, the narrow gauge railway crosses the road (with gates this time so some health and safety progress!) and proceeds behind the photographer towards Cox Lane bridge. A pile of prefabricated track panels lies alongside.

* According to J B Latham in 'The History of McAlpine Steam Locomotives 1869-1965 with List of Contracts', privately published, one locomotive belonging to Sir Alfred McAlpine was used for this contract: No 33, an 0-6-0ST built by Hudswell Clarke in 1913. It was subsequently used at Admiralty sidings at Corsham in 1941/2 and subsequently passed to the NCB at Norton Hill in 1947 - per George Cohen. The engine was finally sold to C Whitlock at Wapping Wharf, Bristol in February 1951 for scrap.

MICHELDEVER AND BASINGSTOKE

Absolutely nothing to do with Chessington, but an interesting contribution from Nigel Barnes-Evans. Early staff views are of course always fascinating, but why has a 10/- stamp, franked as seen, been issued from Micheldever? Suggestions would be welcome.

Nigel has also supplied this view, some information and questions answered but, as is often the case, more are raised. In his own words, "I have recently bought a good quality photograph, dated 1928, showing staff from Basingstoke East signal box. I bought it from the grandson of one of those in the picture. Obviously studio posed and taken by a local photographer it is very sharp and well posed. All eight staff are in full uniform and one wonders why it was taken? The clarity is such that it is possible to read the various staff cap badge numbers.....so would anyone have access to a staff list from the period to identify the others present? The small 'x' (top right) is over the head of Bill Mortimer, the relative referred to, I was told Bill had started at Micheldever, then took a position at Basingstoke".

Plenty to report on this time (having skimped a little on 'Letters and Comments' for the last couple of issues). So to start with a note of nostalgia from Les Burberry reference 'Special Issue No 9 - Scrapping the Southern': "At the time the O2s were being scrapped by H B Joliffe Ltd,(registered office Somerton Works, West Cowes), I enquired as to the cost of purchasing one of the engines. The reply was '£850 or £550 without brass''. Any small change anybody......?

Now to David Lindsell of Andover also on 'Scrapping the Southern, "Just one point concerning the caption of photo at Andover on page 84. Looks to me as No 73169 is reversing out of the yard. Presumably the train would have come from Salisbury and set back into the yard to allow fast trains to pass.".

Next (with an apology) to Alan Postlethwaite who had the lead article on 'Southern Coal' in issue No 26. "The Erith caption has been inadvertently omitted (p22). The caption is as follows: *To meet the ever-growing demand for Newcastle coal in the South-east, **Erith Coal Wharf** opened around 1900. Its rail connection faced south towards Slade Green. It superseded Cray Coal Wharf just to the north of here whose rail connection faced north by Erith passenger station. Both wharves were owned by Cory. There are 208 wagons, two industrial shunters and a dozen barges in this photograph from ca 1930. Bexley Local Studies & Archive Centre.*"

Now from Chris Heaps who sent the accompanying images: "I believe that John Raggett has omitted a further level crossing with gates from his list of ten crossings - that at School Road, Hythe, which is situated only yards from my elder daughter's house. It is not only a rare survivor on the former Southern Railway but was actually installed by the Southern Railway when the Fawley branch opened on 20 July 1925. The branch had been constructed under a Light Railway Order so that most road crossings were open crossings without gates and, at the date of the opening, the School Lane crossing was one of only two gated crossings on the line. In recent years, most public road crossings have been upgraded to automatic half-barriers, but the gates at

School Road are still opened and closed manually. In the last two or three years, new gates have been manufactured and installed and look very smart.

A rare, if not unique, feature of the Hythe Road crossing is that the construction of the line required the demolition of part of an adjoining house - 25 School Road - and the area removed can clearly be seen in the accompanying photograph. Despite being built as a Light Railway, the Inspecting Officer saw no reason why ordinary locomotives should not be used on the line, and today goods services to and from Fawley are hauled by EWS Class 66s, an example of which - No. 66204 - I photographed at the crossing on 2 September 2013 hauling a loaded train from Fawley."

Now about the solution to something I have indeed been wondering, the answer kindly provided by Brian Lawes: "SW No 22 Page 91, the Basingstoke snow plough. It is dumb-buffered because when propelled into a drift, the leading end beam would be lowered using a block and tackle from the swivellable beam on top. This would then form a continuous surface for the snow to pass over.

And in SW No 24 page 59 on the water tank/tender. There are a couple of other uses tenders were put to. One was as a water tank for Permanent Way or Heavy Lifter cranes when they were used on a long weekend job such as bridge renewals and there was no water handy to refill the crane. The other use was in the 1950s for water supply for Ropley station house and offices. Ropley is on the side of a hill and was reputed to have the deepest well in the village. When I used Ropley for school journeys to Winchester two tenders stood in the end unloading dock behind the old signal box site and every so often one went off for refilling. There was a water supply which had reached the top of Ropley station approach by 1947 but that was the end of the main. Eventually someone obviously had found the money to couple the house and offices to the main by the time the goods yard was abolished."

No 70004 at Herne Bay - see letter from Bob Radcliffe overleaf.

Now from Jeremy Clarke, "Re SW 25 Jeremy Clarke Hi Kevin. When convenient will you please make a slight clarification to the caption for the lower photo on p89? (The fault is mine!) At the time the picture was taken the train was travelling on the <u>down relief</u> line which became a reversible one with the signalling change mentioned."

Jeremy continues, "Hello again Kevin, Just a quick note to let you know that a photo and a line drawing of two different (one petrol-driven) Southern Vacuum Cleaning vans are to be found in the excellent reference volume from the Oakwood Press: *Service Stock of the Southern Railway* by RW Kidner. It is an invaluable source of information and illustrations for modellers of the Southern and its former constituent companies. I bought a s/h copy from Amazon for £7 – it's the best £7 I've spent in a long time!"

Now an appeal from Alan Wickens, "Keith *(I think he means Kevin),* first good to see my poster appearing in Issue 25! Second, as we all get older there are times when we look back at occasions that remain in the memory but from which details are lost. My loco-spotting records were destroyed by my late father thinking that 'O' levels were more important than chasing steam engines! I was just wondering with all your contacts, is there someone who might have, for instance, the locos at Ashford works on the open day in 1958? The records I would dearly like to get back are my old school (Skinner's Company in Tunbridge Wells) trip when we did a north London shed bash in 1960, including riding on an 8F on to a turntable at Willesden, culminating in Stratford! Any help appreciated!" *(Any offers….? Alan - your letter was the reason why we included some views of 1950s spotters in this issue.)*

The subject of 'Britannia' class locomotives on the Kent coast lines has started an interesting thread, first another contribution from Jeremy Clarke: " Hi Kevin. May I add my two-pennorth to Tony Francis's very interesting question about a 'Brit' on the Kent Coast line? It is distinctly possible in view of the allocation of two of the class to Stew Lane. But I doubt it occurred regularly simply because of the weight restrictions that applied. I have always been given to understand - and I'm open to correction - that the MNs were not permitted east of Swanley. For this reason - I hope - the heavy up 'Night Ferry' train, which regularly used the ex-Chatham route from Dover, was almost invariably headed post-WW2 by a 'Light Pacific' and a 4-4-0.

"An MN in original condition had an overall weight of 94t 15c and a maximum axleload of 21t. The 'Brit' was about the same, 94t and 20.5t respectively. However, the BR7 was a two-cylinder engine with the endemic problems of balancing and hammer-blow that the 3-cylinder layout of the MN did much to reduce. The same might be applied to the 3-cylinder 'Schools' which were regular performers over the route despite a 21t axleload though overall, of course, much lighter engines at 67t. The 'Arthurs'

One for the signal engineers. The location is clearly Shortlands - but why the apparent 'blanked' green glass in the semaphore spectacles...?

also featured strongly on it, another 2-cylinder engine but with a 20t axleload and overall weight not far short of the Pacifics at 80t 19c (1926 NB batch).

The conclusion then has to be that the sighting was by no means impossible but only occurred either by (a) special dispensation as a 'one-off' or (b) a lack of awareness about the weight restrictions on the part of those who should have known. Be interesting to see what conclusions other correspondents may come to."

Bob Radcliffe adds as follows: "Dear Kevin,
I refer to 'Rebuilt', p.14 of number 25 of Southern Way. Shakespeare and the Duke certainly did appear on the Chatham road in the fifties, and there is photographic evidence in that respect. Dr Ransome Wallis took a beauty of 70004 at Herne Bay, working Stewarts Lane duty 13, the 1.10pm ex Ramsgate, and I have a copy of that. I've also seen a shot of a 'Britannia' on the Arrow at Canterbury East, and I have one of my own - a very poor shot - at Fort Pitt Tunnel, Rochester on the 'up' Ostend boat train which was booked via Chatham on summer Saturdays, so Tony Francis's dad was right!

Going back now to the lower picture on p.72 of SW 23, the head code shown [on positions 2 and 3] is that for a train routed via Selhurst and Beckenham, one of the many variations between London and Dover and occasionally used for boat trains. The normal Victoria to Dover via Orpington and Tonbridge code used brackets 4 and 6, and on the 'Britannias' these were extended. I have been told that this was to stop the lamps blowing out at

speed, which had happened on the 'Arrow' and had resulted in a 'Stop and Examine' procedure.

Another odd code to be seen occasionally on boat trains was on brackets 1 and 5 which, on the western section, was Waterloo to Plymouth! On the Eastern section this was Victoria and Dover/Folkestone via Swanley, Otford and Tonbridge. The official 'Engine Head Signals' book circulated from Deepdene in December 1943 showed no less than thirty-three different permutations for the Central and Eastern Sections alone."

On the same topic from Peter Clark, "With reference to page 114 of The Southern Way issue 25, I can tell you with absolute confidence that both 70004 and 70014 worked boat trains via Chatham.

For the first ten years of my life (1946-1956) I lived in Tonford Lane, Thanington (south west of Canterbury) which was in sight of the Canterbury West-Ashford and Canterbury East-Faversham sections.

These were respectively known locally as the 'Bottom Line' and the 'Top Line' because the first followed the valley of the River Stour and the second ran on embankments as it climbed out of Canterbury towards Selling. A favourite spot was where they crossed at what we called Whitehall or 'The Junction'. This was Whitehall Road which ran close to the SER line and passed over it at Whitehall crossing before briefly splitting in two to pass both under and over the erstwhile Elham Valley line at Harbledown Junction; there was a very low bridge here and another level crossing whose gates remained long after the line was lifted, although in about 1955 a chain link fence took their place. I used to sit on the gates and watch the trains.

The road then passed under the LCDR line and behind Canterbury Junction 'B' signal box at the lower end of the Canterbury loop. Please forgive the detail; I am having a severe attack of nostalgia! *(Don't stop, this is great - Ed.)*

Anyhow, in the summer of 1954 (I think) a 'Britannia' used to work the 2.30 p.m. Dover Marine-Victoria boat train which always included Pullman car *Scotia* and we called this the 3 o'clock boat as this was about the time it passed 'The Junction'. I well remember that *Iron Duke* was the first Britannia I saw and thought it must be an American engine as I had seen nothing like it before. Rebuilt Bulleids and Standard Class 5s were still in the future. As I was not at school, it must have been during the summer holiday. Later on, possibly the same year (the evenings were still light), the up 'Golden Arrow' was routed via Chatham and this would come through Canterbury at about 6.45 p.m.

I first saw *William Shakespeare* on the 'Arrow'; near my house was a footbridge over the river from where I could look across the fields towards 'The Junction'. As soon as the 'Arrow' came into view I would run or cycle as quickly as possible over Tonford crossing on the SER line and up to the LCDR overbridge for a close up view; this was only about half a mile but it was a race to be in time to see the Britannia which was rapidly accelerating by then. Happy days! (In *British Railways Past and Present No. 20 – Kent and East Sussex* – there is a photograph taken by Dr. P. Ransome-Wallis of 70004 on a Ramsgate-Victoria train at Herne Bay; no precise date is given but it is described as being in the early 1950s.)
I am sorry that these are mere childhood memories but assure you they are true. Another is of looking out for the up 'Night Ferry' first thing in the morning when it was worked by the diesel 10203. Best wishes and here's to the next 25 issues of SW.

Now from Richard Derry: "Subject: Issue No.25. Having just purchased the above from the book shop on Minehead station it was nice to see the article on the 'Bournemouth Belle'.

In the early 1960s it was a train that at times governed myself and my fellow spotters' lives. Most of us attended Walton-on-Thames Boys School (now a housing estate) even though we lived in Weybridge. At school we had two sittings for lunch on alternate weeks. On the first sitting we had time to cycle to Hersham Station five minutes away, much closer to school than Walton station. Once at the station we'd leave our bikes on a large heap of others left by commuters and ascend the long stairway to the up platform. To reach the down platform required a walk under the line and the use of another steep staircase. Both platforms were wooden built and the staff tolerated us as they knew we had to be back at school before 1.30pm.

Our main objective was to see the 'Belle' due about 12.50pm and always headed by an immaculate Nine Elms 'Merc' though by now we'd cleared the 70A line up of 'Mercs', hence we wanted to 'spot' the Pullmans. However we were lucky to get half the names/numbers down of the Pullmans. We never had a set pattern, just try and remember some of them. I still have my Ian Allan ABCs with half of the Pullmans underlined. Other highlights at lunchtimes at Hersham would be the occasional E5000 on the down slow or a class W 2-6-4T light engine on transfer, also on the down slow. Or when nobody was looking a friend would put an old penny on the up slow running line and retrieve it after it had been run over by a local emu."

Richard continues about the 'Belle', "On Saturdays or during school holidays, dry mornings would be spent at the local spotting place, 'Haines Bridge' or if wet, under shelter at Weybridge Station which still has an enclosed footbridge - Happy Days. Lunchtime was governed by the passing of the 'Belle', hopefully a different Merc to that seen mid-week and the usual panic to try and 'cop' a few Pullmans, and then it was home for lunch. Less than two minutes walk from Haines Bridge we'd be halfway along the woodland path overlooking the cutting that leads to Weybridge station when the Belle passed, so we wouldn't be late for lunch. Of course it passed here a few minutes after passing Hersham station, normally 12.55pm at Weybridge station.

The up train of the early evening passed under Haines Bridge at 6.20pm and what with tea followed by homework we were lucky to see the Belle at this time and when it appeared, it was going at a good speed. The Pullmans were not easy to note but then we had other movements on our minds, especially the two down Nine Elms to Southampton goods worked by 70B based S15s and the challenge to count the number of wagons. We never agreed on the total and always got lost after 50!"

Most recently a grovelling apology from me over my note to the cover of Issue No 26. This is from Richard Bell but others have voiced a similar note about the cover. "This cannot possibly be unit 4356: the series 4355 to 4387 were all new-build steel-bodied units produced in 1947-48. I think it must be 4506, the second with that number, formed in 1956 and withdrawn in January 1960.

In 1956 the 4 EPB construction programme was nearing its end, and few 4 SUB units with cars having pre-grouping bodywork remained. However, 72 such cars were rounded up and used to make up 18 units numbered 4501-4518. These units were to be a stop-gap while the 2 Nol units were withdrawn. Their underframes and bogies were reconditioned, new SR-style steel bodies were produced (the last ones) and new traction equipments were procured to create 2 HAP units 5601-5636 (in 1957-58) and then 2 EPB 5651-5684 (for Waterloo-Staines-Windsor/Weybridge services, in 1959).

All but three of these cars were originally in 3-car motor units in the series 1717-1772 produced in 1929-30, prime examples of the SR's skill at recycling. Bodies and underframes came from LBSC-designed a.c. CP and CW trailers and driving trailers, lengthened on conversion to the standard 62', employing also LBSCR trailing bogies, so that only the d.c. motor bogies and traction equipments were wholly new.

The three exceptions had ex-a.c. frames and trailing bogies but LSWR bodywork and were initially in 3-car units 1780 and 1781 of 1930. Under the 1939 stock reorganization and replacement program the ex-a.c. underframes were not to be re-used, and it was probably intended that the 3-car units containing such cars were not to be augmented, but withdrawn as they were near the end of the programe. The war of course disrupted these plans.

Most of the 3-car units were augmented in 1949 with steel trailers, some new and some from units augmented earlier and disbanded, and as 4 SUB units were numbered in the range 4527 and 4574. In 1956 the steel trailers were taken for inclusion in 4 EPB units 5216-5260 (requiring electrical modifications), and therefore the reformed units 4501-4517 each included two wooden-bodied trailers and contained cars from at least two previous units. Unit 4518 was a renumbering of 4251, formed in 1944 from 3-car unit 1736 with an LBSCR-bodied trailer from a disbanded unit.

Page 35. I suspect that this view of an almost deserted London Bridge was taken at around 2pm on a summer Sunday afternoon. The train headcode 75 is a clue. Bexleyheath line trains went beyond Dartford only on Sundays, and this train would be bound for Gravesend. The only regular through workings between London and Maidstone West were the portions detached from/attached to the regular hourly Gillingham semi-fasts via Woowich

Arsenal at Strood, always at the up end of the trains, which showed headcodes 82/83 going down. The headcodes 46/47, 56/57, 64/65, 74/75, 84/85 therefore in practice unambiguously identified down trains to Gravesend."

From Mike King: "Regarding the picture of the Devon Belle observation saloon on the latest SW; I have a picture of the stock at Winchester City, travelling "up" which I have been asked about before. My notes on the reverse suggest that this was a private charter, possibly on 8 July 1951, for visitors to Romsey Abbey and Winchester Cathedral. As the Devon Belle ran only on certain days of the week (Friday, Saturday, Sunday, Monday normally but at times including a down Thursday and an up Tuesday trip, Wednesdays were always the days when the set would be available for private hire - however 8 July 1951 was a Sunday so not sure what this proves!!

Now an interesting snippet from Kevin Darkin: "Just been reading SW No 23. In September 1963 a school friend and I saw a 9F with a Tyesley 2A shed plate (we also saw Light Pacifics with Exmouth Junction 83D shedplates). The 9F was on a west of England bound freight at Salisbury. In October 1964 we also saw a "Britannia" on a London bound special at Fratton.

Straying from this on an SR theme, a correspondent in the April Railway Magazine mentions an SR scheme to electrify the West of England main line with 1500 volts DC. I admit I have never heard this before. Do your readers know of any SR schemes to extend electrification beyond Pirbright Junction to either Bournemouth or Exeter (or beyond)?" *(I am sure I have heard of this but can someone help with the detail - Ed?)*

Left and opposite - three colour images recently acquired but without detail of locations. Thanks then to Christopher Fifield for coming up with answers even before we went to print! "Left looks like Petts Wood, the down 'Goldlen Arrow' behind a BB. Opposite top: Redhill, a down Victoria - Brighton semi-fast formed of two 4 LAV units. Bottom right is Tonbridge with an MLV leading an up boat train."

A design typical of the Southern, the go-anywhere, do anything 'Mogul'. At home on all but the fastest or heaviest trains examples of the type could be seen from 'Kent to Cornwall'. This example is 'N' No 31401 taking the Guildford line south at Woking, (which, together with the extract underneath [for which many thanks to Gerry Nichols] leads us very nicely into what follows on the page opposite.... .).

Memorandum of Visit to Templecombe and Bournemouth Central, Thursday 28 October 1937.

Present: Mr G S Szlumper General manager. Mr E J Missenden Traffic Manager, Mr G Ellson Chief Engineer, Mr W H Shortt Divisional Engineer*, Mr A Cobb Locomotive Running Superintendent**, Mr E Hight Divisional Superintendent** Mr A B Chester Divisional Engineer**. (* = present at Templecombe only, ** = present at Bournemouth Central only.

1.Templecombe. An inspection was made of the works carried out. It is anticipated that the whole of the new station buildings will be completed in time for next Summer's train service. It is understood that the provision of the new station name boards is being pursued by the Public Relations and Advertising Officer. The General Manager raised the question of the provision of loud-speaker apparatus; this to be considered and reported upon by the Divisional Superintendent.

2. Bournemouth Central.

(a) Modernisation. Consideration was given to the under mentioned modernisation proposals, which were approved; the scheme to be submitted to the General Manager.

Improvements to artificial lighting and necessary alterations

to water services. £328

Forming Silence Cabinet to enclosed telephones in Down Side Enquiry Office, alterations to glazing of windows, providing shelf for telegrams in Booking Hall, removing brickwork and extending railing around top of subway on Down Platform and sundries, including providing two new Ticket Collectors' boxes. £155

Modern pedestals and stalls and tiling walls to Gentlemens Courts and W.C.s on both platforms including removing screen and bricking up rear entrance to Up Side Court. £895

New Cycle Shed on Up platform and tidying bank supporting parcels yard. £50

Improving seating in Waiting Rooms, mirrors and receptacles in Ladies Lavatories and teak seats in Down Side Booking Hall. £270.

New Platform seats. £165.

Re-arranging advertising display, nameplates, signs, etc., matchboarding surfaces for advertising purposes and providing additional boards. £832.

Total £2,695

The Southern Railway from Inception to Nationalisation and beyond

Part 6: Great Progress in very difficult times

(They called it the "Slump" in the 1930's, today it is an "Economic Crisis")

Alan Blackburn (continuing the series started by Tony Goodyear)

When I visited Tony in The Woking Hospice for what was to be the last time, I asked him if there was anything I could do for him. I expected perhaps some social duty or what have you, so I was more than a little surprised when he asked me to finish this series of articles.

We had both worked in Southern House at Croydon, the HQ of the Southern Region's technical departments. Tony worked in the S&T Drawing Office, I in the P-Way Drawing Office. Tony and I had plenty of time for conversation as we frequently commuted together, we were both EM gauge railway modellers and, more to the point we both believed that the Southern Railway was without doubt the finest railway this country had ever seen and quite possibly the best it ever will see.

One's early childhood days are very formative and in the 1940s our house overlooked the railway at Havant with a good view of all that passed. There were the Electrics of course, then almost brand new but I don't think I knew that then: as for "The Hayling Billy", nothing very unusual about that!

Far more interesting to a young boy were the Goods trains: these were the freights working between Eastleigh and Chichester and beyond. These brought the big Urie engines with their massive bogie tenders, the handsome Brighton Ks and a whole variety of lesser fry; Hoppers, Black Motors, Vulcans and their poor relatives the C3s and Radials. Not that I knew their nick-names then; that had to wait for my first Ian Allan ABC. Seen only once was the 'Hornby'(CC1) running light engine to Fratton; and again once only, a USA 2-8-0, painted, I remember, in a funny shade of "greenish" grey. Then of course there were the 'Charlies' (Q1s) which I was told were also American - one lives and learns, as they say. Funny thing, if these engines were amongst your earliest recollections then there was nothing strange about their appearance. They were part of the everyday scene and that was that.

So that was by way of introduction and I will now do my best to follow Tony's lead. He referred in his last article to the main line electrification and I will of course deal with that, but first I think I had better mention the standard SR steam-hauled passenger and freight stock, as these were very much on the scene before the Brighton line electrification.

As I am sure you all know, one referred to "Maunsell stock" because he was the Chief Mechanical Engineer when they were built but he, of course, did not design the vehicles; that was done by small a team of C&W design staff led by who? That is a good question that has been never fully explained.

The Assistant Mechanical Engineer (Carriages,

Perhaps the most typical of SR goods wagons, the Covered Goods - as restored by the Bluebell. The brown might be a little on the light side but it soon faded in service.

Top - 2 BIL No 2069 as running in later years with a Bulleid profile HAL trailer. Note the tail lamp on the nearside lamp iron: in Southern days the passenger train tail lamps were always in this position. If the nearside was not alongside the platform then you had to go through the cab. SR 'heritage lines' please note!
P J Sharpe

Opposite bottom - No 23 'Totland' in Ryde Yard with A B MacLeod himself on the footplate. The engine still has LSWR lamp-irons which were replaced shortly afterwards by standard SR type in order that 15-inch headcode discs could be carried.
O J Morris

Wagons and Road Vehicles) was Surrey Warner who had held the same position with the South Western. Under him at Eastleigh was a small but very competent Drawing Office team, led by one W H Beckley. Over at Lancing there was a similar team led by a Mr. H Thorpe; he was quite young and there was nothing Lancing could teach Eastleigh about design. Now we come to Lionel Lynes. He had headed up the C&W design team at Ashford. A Great Western man by training, he was one of the new team brought to Ashford by Maunsell back in 1914, following Wainwright's departure. Lynes was junior to Mr. Beckley, but Maunsell brought him to Waterloo in 1924 as one of his small team of personal assistants as we might best describe them: all South Eastern men. Lionel Lynes' title was that of Senior Carriage and Wagon Draughtsman.

Now we know that many at Eastleigh were not best pleased by this situation. That their old chief Robert Urie had chosen to retire was understandable, as was the choice of Maunsell as his successor, but what of these other South Eastern people up there at Waterloo? Was Mr. Beckley not senior in grade and service to this chap Lynes and was the South Western not senior to the South Eastern in all other respects?

It may well be that Beckley was happy to remain in his own office surrounded by people he knew; and that Maunsell likewise wanted someone in this key position that he already knew and trusted, perhaps not even thinking or knowing of Beckley and Thorpe. Like a lot of other things we will probably never know the facts behind this situation.

What I can say, having been privileged to work in a HQ Office is that the head of a railway department, no matter what department, has a tremendous amount of policy, admin. and committee work to get through. He doesn't get to design anything and anyway design is only a comparatively small part of the total workload in an

engineering department, dominated as it is by maintenance. The chief might, if he is interested in some particular aspect of what is going on, give the relevant section leader guidance of what he would like to see done and he might sign some of the more important drawings, otherwise everything is delegated down to its appropriate level.

I am sure Maunsell knew more about his Departmental Budget and what he was expected to do with it than anything else. His successor, Mr. Bulleid, of course was another man entirely and he must have had an incredibly good team of clerical people to keep him out of trouble.

But where were we? Yes, the organisation of the Southern's C&W design team etc. Well, for what it is worth, I think Surrey Warner in his office at Eastleigh was fully employed running a greatly enlarged department; and so far as construction was concerned he was probably more concerned with the production of the electric suburban stock than anything else. One can imagine him thinking that it was a pity about Mr Beckley missing out, but Maunsell had this chap Lynes with him and he seems to know what he is doing.

Over at Ashford, this young man Lynes had recently designed some sound if rather unusual and lengthy boat train stock and had followed that with what we enthusiasts call the Thanet stock etc. Irrespective of the bodywork, all these vehicles had a similar modern underframe and a good simple bogie.

In the works there, the carriage body Foremen, in conjunction with their drawing office colleagues, were busy assembling electric suburban stock from old steam-hauled vehicles, a job that called for a lot of practical knowledge and experience. They knew their own stock like the back of their hands but they must have struggled when it came to dealing with the Brighton and South Western vehicles of

Top - Just to prove to Eastleigh men (who had no time for the class) that a 'Q' could handle more than a 3-set: AND the engine is blowing off! No 30531 is on a Ramblers' excursion from Victoria and has just passed the up marker-light for Selham, 15 October 1950. (Selham station is in the background.)
S C Nash

which they had no experience, and here they must have had to rely heavily on the respective drawing offices, a task not helped by the fact that Brighton coaches did not always agree with their records and drawings. Sorry, if you are a Brighton enthusiast, but that was the truth of the matter and as Eastleigh found out later it applied to engines as well!

So what was Mr. Lynes doing up there at Waterloo? Well, according to an article he wrote for the Locomotive Magazine he conceived the basic requirements of what was required whilst lying in his bath!

Exactly to what detail he followed this through we will never know, but I guess that having gone through all the relevant diagrams, what he meant was that he figured out a need for a brake third with two sizes of brake van, a brake compo, a compo, a third and a first. All would be built as required to three basic body widths: 9ft, 8ft 6ins and 8ft wide - the last two to suit the sub-standard clearances on certain old SE&CR lines. The various dining car requirements, nondescript saloons, passenger vans etc etc probably came later. All were to have the same 57ft underframe equipped with toilets, Pullman corridor connections and "buck-eye" couplings.

I think one can be reasonably sure he had a long quiet look at the South Western 'Ironclads', that he looked around at what the other three main line Companies were doing; and he then sketched up some guidelines for the drawing office at Eastleigh, for them to work up the details. They after all were going to build the bodies and they would

Top - *Former 'City Limited' set No 3042, running ECS from New Cross Gate to Victoria, seen approaching Crystal Palace LL.R C Riley*

Bottom - *U1 No 899 at Waterloo on what may be a Portsmouth express. (Two discs either side of the smokebox is in the book but that seen is not.) It seems that great things were expected of the U1s but their performance was not up to that of the other Maunsell Mogul's. They could run alright so long as they had enough steam but it would seem the boiler was simply not big enough for a three-cylinder engine travelling at speed. No shed kept them any longer than they had to. At Fratton the men preferred the Drummond D15s they had been originally intended to replace, whereas the Schools were in a different league altogether.*

have to produce the many production drawings required to enable this to be done.

I should at this point mention that as early as October 1923 it had been decided that Eastleigh would build the majority of new carriage bodies, whilst Lancing would build the remainder and all new underframes. Ashford would build wagons. Not mentioned at the time this was announced but as we have already mentioned, Ashford was also given the massive job of providing most of the stock required for the suburban electrification. This was probably because most of the early conversions were ex-South Eastern, and South Eastern and Chatham Railway stock.

Lancing had really no experience of designing modern carriages, although they had built some of the Eastleigh-designed 'Ironclads', and some of the Ashford-designed 'Thanet' stock. Lancing had a competent drawing office of course and they quite likely were given the job of developing the standard SR carriage underframe as Lancing was going to build most of them. This underframe followed the Lynes' SE&CR designs closely, the most important difference being that all the underframes destined for corridor steam stock were equipped with a three-quarter-sized version of the American 'Buck-eye' coupling that hung on a normal hook and could be dropped when it was necessary to couple to a non-buck-eye vehicle. Three–quarter-sized it might be, but it was heavy enough to handle, I can tell you from personal experience, and no joke for those who were not used to them. If you want to see what the full-size version looks like, have a look at the Mendip stone wagons.

So far as the bodywork of a Maunsell carriage goes, I would simply say that it was a good-looking vehicle, very well thought out, and in fact very much a set of assembled standard parts. The vans with their vertical sides required for the Guard's lookout were unusual, a matter dictated by the loading gauge, of course. When I showed my old friend, the late Ray Chorly, round the Bluebell C&W shops and mentioned how much we would have liked a typical Maunsell 3-set, he said, as one who had worked his way up from the shop floor at Lancing to become a C&W designer, "Well, why don't you build one? You have got suitable underframes, you have the skill, everything else is an assembly of parts".

Lancing held all these standard parts in stock: "If you needed anything, say to replace a damaged door pillar for instance, you simply went into the stores and they gave you one." He also mentioned, incidentally, that he only saw a drawing on the shop floor once, and that was when a badly-damaged EMU front end needed rebuilding. Otherwise those concerned knew what they were doing from experience.

I am not going into any detail concerning the Maunsell carriages and will simply say that the subject has been covered very well by the books of David Gould and Mike King. Returning to the question of the guard's lookout, I do not know what the other railways did but on the Southern the guard was expected to assist the driver with the observance of signals. I never heard of a Guard who prevented a "run-by" but there it was, one of those rules very hard to observe. A further point worth mentioning perhaps is that the guard was in charge of the train and not, as many think, the driver. The driver was responsible for what he and his fireman did with the engine.

Sorry, I have wandered, I fear that I might do that quite often.

So far as passenger vans were concerned the four-wheeled vans designed by Lynes for the SE&CR set the general style, the bodywork having more in common with his goods vans than your average passenger vehicle. Over on the South Eastern they referred to these vans as "Nurse Cavell" vans, as the first one built was used to bring that lady's remains to London for burial. Personally I never heard these vans referred to as anything other than a "U van". They had one big failing, they had no internal lighting so after dark everything in them had to be sorted with the aid of a hand lamp.

An interesting aside. The underframes of the SE&CR-built vans lacked the usual diagonal frame members normally found behind the headstocks on a British railway vehicle, this omission was corrected on all later batches, all that is except for a batch built at Wolverton in BR days. It would seem that Wolverton was sent the original underframe drawings (instead of) the revised ones!

A few words about Southern standard goods stock, again a subject covered in some detail elsewhere by the work of Jerry Bixley, Ray Chorly, Mike King and myself. The first standard Southern goods wagon, an 8-plank open goods did not appear until 1926. This wagon was intended, so it has been said, for use as either a mineral wagon or for general goods. Both the South Western and the SE&CR had very similar wagons. Most SR wagons were a development of Lynes' standard SE&CR designs and they in turn followed Swindon practice. The main difference now was the use of the new standard 1923 RCH 17ft 6in underframe. All types had the steel version except the early cattle and stone wagons which had wooden ones for usage reasons.

There followed a covered goods wagon with its distinctive roof which followed the style of the carriage stock. This was said to have been originally designed to obtain a certain cubic loading capacity. I forget now what that was, but the basic shape was a mistake because in later years it gave constant trouble with leaks, What worked well enough on a passenger vehicle could not stand up to the constant "racking" movement that a goods wagon was subjected too. The later plywood-sheeted wagons were much more rigid and therefore better but even they leaked sometimes.

The same roof profile was used for what might have become the standard SR goods brake van, "The Dance Halls". With their generally stronger construction these did not leak but they had no "guard's lookout". This was a basic requirement on the South Western Section that Lynes

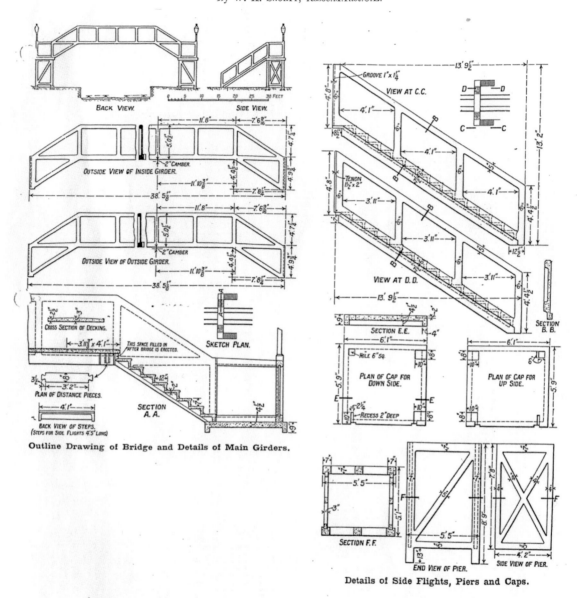

A PRE-CAST FERRO-CONCRETE FOOTBRIDGE.

An Interesting Example of Ferro-Concrete Construction on the Southern Railway.

By W. H. SHORTT, Assoc.M.Inst.C.E.

Outline Drawing of Bridge and Details of Main Girders.

Details of Side Flights, Piers and Caps.

Above - From the 'Railway Engineer', January 1924. This is the early standard concrete footbridge originally designed as a 'like for like' replacement of an earlier LSWR timber footbridge. (Alton has the last of these.) About 1935 the design was replaced by a heavier structure, easier recognised by having three bays in the centre compared with the four shown here. (See image of Hillsea Halt on p52.)

Opposite - This drawing was originally shown in the 'Railway Gazette' for 23 June 1937. These sheds all had much in common as to detail but the centre line of the main verticals varied.

Location	Number of Roads	Vertical centres	Width
West Worthing	3	34'	45'
Farnham	5	30' 3"	77'
Ore	4	40'	60'
Fratton	4	39' 3"	60'
That portrayed may well be Fratton.			

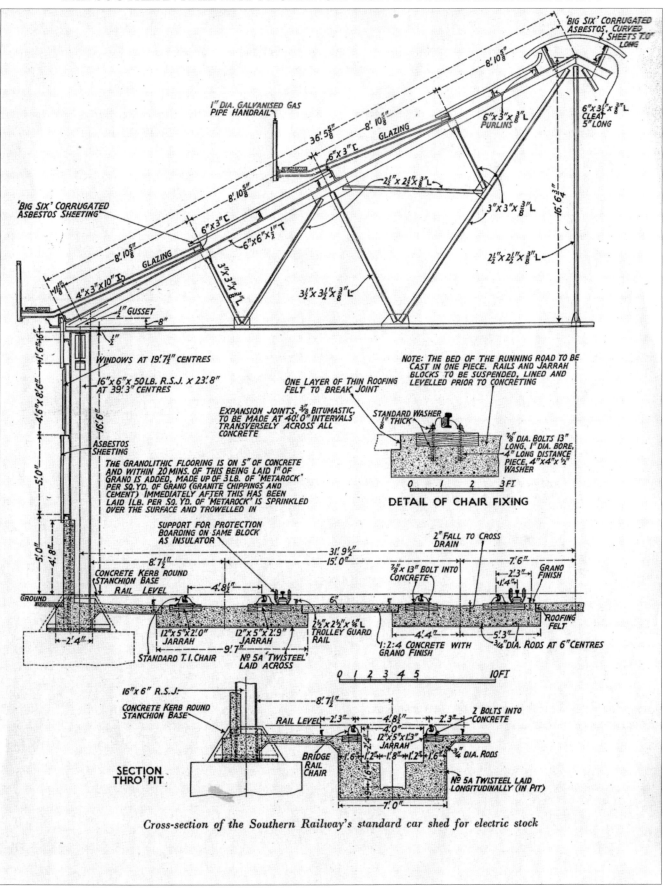

Cross-section of the Southern Railway's standard car shed for electric stock

apparently knew nothing about; the SE&CR did not use them! Moreover questions were asked at a high level as to why such a large body was provided to accommodate one man. The result was the Lancing designed "Pill Box". From the sublime to the ridiculous one might say. As was said, "With a wet mackintosh hanging up in it, it was full"! Another problem with these vans was that the doors opened on to the internal seat, not a good idea. The later vans had a reversed internal layout and that solved the problem but the older vans were never altered.

Another design that got the C&W into trouble was the underframe of the eight bogie wagons built for the Lynton & Barnstaple line in 1927, four opens and four covered goods. These had no sooner entered service than it was discovered that their brake gear fouled some of the line's point rodding. If the line had an agreed Loading Gauge it seems no one east of Exeter knew about it. Correspondence passed between the Chief Civil Engineer at Waterloo and the Divisional Engineer at Exeter, it being a CCE matter, but they knew nothing of any proposed new stock and the end result was that the wagons' brake gear had to be expensively altered as did the covered wagons' body framing later - but that is another story.

Now we have to mention the L&B somewhere so this is as good a place as any. Again, I am not going into any great detail as there are at least ten books on the subject of the L&BR. What though has always puzzled me is not that the line closed in 1935, but why it closed so soon after the Southern had spent a lot of money on it.

For what it is worth I have three theories on the subject.

1.That it was found that the three early Manning Wardle engines all had expensive boiler problems. At auction they fetched no more than their scrap value when one or more might have found a sale for further use as did the later engine the Southern supplied.

2.That a considerable amount of track renewal was required if the line was to continue much longer. That was a stated fact.

3. That following the recent agreement with the bus companies, the Southern figured it would get a fair share of the revenue anyway and perhaps this was the way forward generally, and that this instance would make a good trial. I think I like this theory best or was it a case of all three together?

Well now, perhaps this is the time to consider the Brighton line electrification. The LB&SCR had been threatened with various proposals for a competing line to Brighton over the years, including a scheme at the turn of the Century for a brand new electric railway. It did indeed carry out certain quadrupling works to counter the threat, and had in 1903 obtained Parliamentary powers to electrify the entire system.

The Southern's suburban electrification schemes were arranged so that each followed one another as a rolling program. This kept the key people and experience together so when the suburban system was largely finished, it was no great surprise that Sir Herbert Walker announced at the 1930 AGM that the Brighton main line was going to be electrified.

Up until this time the money for the various electrification schemes had been found by the Southern from its own resources and care was taken to ensure that suburban electrification went hand in hand with house construction. The lessons of "Metroland" were well understood at Waterloo.

This time it was different and the money was going to be provided by the Government under a scheme to promote railway modernisation and above all to provide work. The country was then in a very similar financial and employment situation to that in which we find ourselves today, except that, give or take a few of the smaller builders going bankrupt, suburban house construction in the South East had continued unabated.

This time there would be no commuters to guarantee the success of the scheme, at least not enough of them at first, so it was a little bit of a risk but as always Sir Herbert Walker knew what he was doing and he had the entire Board behind him. The Southern Railway Board never took a decision unless it was unanimous.

Power was to be taken for the first time from what became known as the National Grid and advantage was to be taken of developments in the track-side power supply system that enabled the sub-stations to be remotely controlled from a central location, in this case Three Bridges. This saved a lot of expensive manpower, as most of the previous sub-stations had to be manned around the clock. It also introduced for the first time that familiar SR sight of the sub-station with its outdoor transformer and switch gear mounted on elevated concrete framing. The "TP Hut" or Track Paralleling Hut was another new feature, there being one between each sub-station. These enabled a sub-station to be switched out for maintenance or repair without affecting the train service.

The actual track to be electrified was from Coulsdon North to Brighton and along the West Coast line to West Worthing and included the first few miles of the Guildford line from Redhill to Reigate. The Quarry line, and from Stoats Nest to Brighton, 36 miles, was converted to mostly three-, but with a few four-aspect colour-light signals, making it the longest stretch of colour-light signalling in the country.

Work commenced in 1931 and public services commenced on the 1st of January 1933 - an incredible achievement when one considers the amount of work involved: an entirely new station at Haywards Heath; a new 130-lever mechanical lever frame at Three Bridges, installed whilst the old one continued in use; a new 225-lever power frame installed in a new box at Brighton and brought into

A typical Kent Coast Summer Saturday train seen running through Herne Hill. The Southern found the Stirling 4-4-0s to be among its most efficient locomotives, far better than either the Brighton B2X or Drummond C8 types.

use in just five hours; a rebuilt 12-road car shed at Lovers Walk complete with the Southern's first carriage washing machine; a new 3-road car shed at West Worthing. To this should be added, the re-railing of much of the main line with British Standard rails, the old LBSC ones having fish plates and fish-bolt hole spacing that did not suit the standard SR electrical track bonding. The old rails, being otherwise in good condition, were cascaded to lines not likely to be electrified. One could go on and on with the details but they can all be found elsewhere: suffice to say that by to-day's standards one can only be amazed at what was done in less than two years. The whole scheme, as were all subsequent ones, was brought in slightly under budget and on time.

The rolling stock required fell into two groups: one for the semi-fast services and the other for the fast services. The semi-fast stock consisted of what came to be called the 4-LAVs. Each set consisted of two composite coaches, one with a side corridor giving access to a toilet at each end, flanked by two identical motor brake thirds each with two 275 HP motors as used on the suburban stock. The whole

set was coupled by standard screw couplings and one wonders why buck-eyes were not used as was standard on the contemporary steam stock.

The bodywork was very similar to the current steam stock. The guard's van and driver's cab had the slab sides as usually provided for the guard's duckets, but there were none, for the guard was now provided with a periscope on the roof to observe the signals. Was this a late change of plan? It seems likely since the fast service stock had the conventional tumble home of the 9ft stock. One odd detail was that the corridor compartment doors on these Brighton line carriages consisted of two narrow sliding doors linked together as was common practice on the LMS. There were 33 of these sets with two more Bulleid versions added in 1940.

The fast service stock came in three varieties, each tailor-made for the service to be provided. The biggest batch was 20 six-sets known as 6-PULs. These consisted of a rather good looking motor brake third at each end, each with four 225 HP motors. Their maximum speed was 75mph. At the time it was said that consideration had been

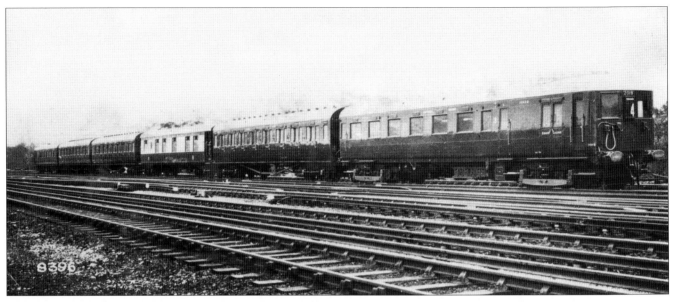

A 6PUL recorded when brand-new. From the front end the order is, Motor brake-third, Composite, Pullman First, Composite, Third and finally another Motor brake-third. The white painted ends of the conductor rails may be noted.

given to the use of electric locomotives and one wonders about the evolution of these vehicles because they might well have been described as small electric locomotives carrying passenger accommodation! (See SW No 20 p55.) They certainly rode like locomotives and in fact one was used in a trial to haul thirty-odd wagons from New Cross Gate to Three Bridges. A K class steam engine trailed the train throughout but apparently all went well. The rest of the train was composed of conventional coaches although they did have non-standard compensated 9ft-wheelbase bogies. These carriages consisted of a third, two compos and a first-class Pullman, the latter to replace the Pullman cars included in so many of the old Brighton main line steam trains.

Then there were the six-set 6 CITYs: motor coaches as before but the trailers were all firsts. These sets were a direct replacement of the old Brighton City Limited. Finally there were the well known 5 BELs, to make up an all-Pullman train consisting of two motor brake thirds, a third and two firsts.

The Brighton line electrification very quickly established itself as a great success and extensions to Eastbourne and along the East Coast line to Hastings followed in 1935, including Brighton to Lewes and Newhaven, and, rather interestingly, Haywards Heath to Horsted Keynes. From which one must conclude that Waterloo was thinking even then of a second electric route to Brighton that avoided the Balcombe Viaduct. It is not likely that you have stood on Balcombe viaduct whilst a train passes, but I have and the vibration and general movement is alarming, to say the least of it; but then I am not a Bridge Engineer.

These later routes required 17 six-sets known as 6-PANs. These were as the 6-PULs but had a first class trailer

instead of the Pullman, incorporating a pantry compartment for light refreshments: again, the make-up was tailored to the service. The bogies under the trailer coaches reverted to the standard SR 8ft-wheelbase steam stock design.

There was now a need for suitable stock for the local services along the coast. This was covered in the short term by the use of 3-SUBs but in due course the 2 NOL was introduced (NOL: No lavatory). These had a 250 HP motor brake third more or less identical to that of a SUB coupled by a SUB's three-link chain and single buffer to a control trailer compo. The bodywork for these units was taken from former L&SWR compartment steam stock. They were not wonderful but they did the job and there were eventually 93 of them, being also used in due course on the Portsmouth, Alton and Windsor line services.

Conceived at about the same time were the 2 BILs (Bi- or two lavatory) units. These were all new and were formed like the NOLs with a 250 HP motor brake third and a driving compo. These were probably the most comfortable of all the SR electric stock, the seating was superb and the ride reasonable. Again they were destined to be used in a similar way to the NOLs and frequently worked with them. There were eventually 152 of these fine units, the first ten differing in detail from the later units. I guess they were not supposed to exceed 50mph but like the "Nelsons" (later) they would run like the wind downhill!

That, I think, is enough about "Juicers" for the time being: but it was they that made the Southern's profits and one must remember that the Southern Railway was above all else a superbly-run, very large, business. I hope I am not going to bore you but to make that point I am now going to list the various Departments of that business as it was in 1935. Here we go - the General Manager's Department, the Company Secretary's Dept, the Solicitor's Dept, Accounts

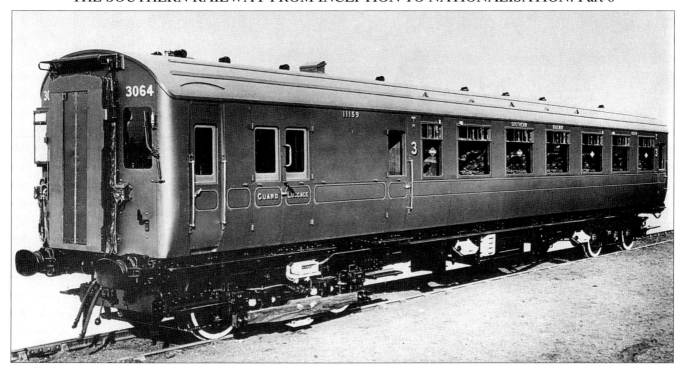

Motor Brake Third No 11159 from 4 COR set No 3064, a good example of 'Lynes' later carriages. The vehicle is seen in Maunsell green with orange and black lining and a light grey roof. The fuse box colour was light grey and the shoe beam, as was Southern practice, has been varnished.

Dept, Audit Accounts Dept, Traffic Dept, (five divisions), Loco Running Dept (two divisions - yes two, Eastern and Western), Engineer's Dept, (six divisions), Mechanical Engineer's Dept, Electrical Dept, Dock and Marine Dept, Stores Dept, The Estate Agent, Police, House Supt, Medical Officers, Foreign and Channel Island Office, the Road Transport Co's Association., all that is before you split the Departments into their sub-sections.

One of the largest and most important areas of the Southern's empire was that of Shipping and Docks. I have in fact seen the Southern described as a Shipping Line with its own Docks and Railway! A whole book could be written on this subject - indeed a book could easily be written on Southampton Docks alone. Already an important passenger port, the Southern more than doubled its capacity to make it the premier passenger port in the country, able to handle (and dry-dock) the largest ships in the world. We tend to forget that in the 1930s and indeed into the early fifties almost everyone, and that includes of course the most important and famous, arrived and left these islands by sea, and more often than not that meant care of the Southern Railway. Those Ocean Liner specials and Continental boat trains were important. It must be said that the latter had a notorious reputation for running late but the reason was usually the weather or more likely delays caused by Customs and Immigration. Some things never change.

Besides Southampton the SR owned dock facilities at no less than 29 other locations; some, such as Deptford Wharf, are now long-forgotten, but once were very busy indeed handling, in that location, mostly coal from the North East and Scandinavian timber.

Turning to ships, I am no expert on this subject but I make the total of ships owned by the SR at one time or another (not counting tugs and barges etc), as no less than 72, with another ten jointly owned with the French (a little under 50 being the average in service at any one time). I have read that they were all superbly maintained and that several were the first in their class with various technical innovations such as stabilisers and manoeuvring aids etc.

We cannot leave the SR shipping world without mention of the train ferry service. This ran between Dover and Dunkirk and started in October 1936, after a heavy delay caused by engineering problems encountered in the construction of the special lock-enclosed dock at Dover. This was necessitated by the considerable difference in tide levels. This service was used, of course, by the "Night Ferry" overnight passenger service from Victoria to Paris Nord . This service was a great gift to the publicity people but I wonder if it ever justified its costs.

The cross-channel goods traffic, especially the fruit traffic from Southern Europe, was another matter, but it has been said that the Southern missed a great opportunity in not continuing the successful goods ferry services set up during the First World War that ran to France from Southampton and Richborough. The passenger service required the very expensive docking facility at Dover needed to make it independent of the state of the tide, whereas a goods service alone would not have needed this. As it was, the three

Above - 'Modern architecture' at Southampton, down side in June 1939. The building would suffer heavy damage from German bombing just 18 months later.

Opposite top - Surbiton as rebuilt in 1937/1938. Perhaps this was the most extreme of the Southern's 'modern style' stations.

Opposite bottom - The down side waiting room at Surbiton on 3 March 1938. Those seats might look modern but boy were they uncomfortable! Not everything was green and cream on the 'modern' SR stations, the waiting room and other platform doors were grained oak with brass kicking plates which had to be kept polished. Note the green dado-rail on the end wall. This was discontinued in early BR days.

2 HAL unit No 2663 forming the front set of the 10.17 am Brighton to Portsmouth Harbour train passing Hilsea Halt on 30 April 1961. Spanning the platforms is a later type Exmouth junction footbridge with three centre-bays. The steel bridge be-yond was a temporary construction bridge originally erected at Farlington Junction in connection with the building of the Eastern Road overbridge. J Courtenay-Haydon

purpose-built ferries and their associated link-spans were sold in 1923 to the "Great Eastern Train Ferry Company" and used from Harwich to Zeebrugge in Belgium, a service that started in 1924 and ran in competition with the Southern. In 1934 it was taken over by the L&NER.

I guess that the nearest many railway enthusiasts got to going to sea was their trips to the Isle of Wight; and yes, the Island boats could roll. I remember on one occasion three warps were broken trying to come alongside at Ryde and eventually we had to go back to Portsmouth because they only had two left! Now I expect most of you must know all about the railways in the Island, at least twenty books have been published on various aspects of this fascinating subject; and when you get there today there is the Isle of Wight Steam railway, for my money the finest standard gauge preserved railway in the country. They do everything well. Am I biased? Well yes, but I stand by what I've just written.

Now, the books will tell you that the Island's first railway was the Cowes & Newport (C&NR), opened on the 16th June 1862: but I would take issue with that because there was a railway serving the Hamstead Estate (near Shalfleet) several years before that. This connected the house by a circular route to a quay on the Newtown creek. I don't know much about it beyond that, but I guess it was built with material supplied by one William Croskill of Beverly. His lines were intended for agricultural use and used gauges of 2ft 6ins and 3ft. He offered a complete range of pre-fabricated track, wagons etc and by 1851 when he exhibited at the Great Exhibition he claimed to have sold over 18000ft of track in 27 countries. I might be wrong about the details but there was certainly an early railway of sorts at Hamstead.

The next line to be built was the Isle of Wight Railway (IWR) which opened from Ryde to Shanklin in 1864 with a short branch to a quay at Brading. This line was extended to the health resort of Ventnor in 1866.

A little out of sequence, but somewhere in the mid-seventies, it is not recorded exactly when, the Brading Harbour Railway, as it was called, extended the line from the IWR branch at Brading to new quays at St Helens and on to Bembridge. This was opened as a passenger railway in 1882 and in 1898 the IWR formally took it over. The third standard gauge railway in the Island was the Isle of Wight & Newport Junction Railway (IW&NJR). This opened from Sandown to Pan Lane, on the outskirts of Newport, in 1875 but was not completed to Newport proper until 1878, the delay being the need for a viaduct the IWNJR could not afford! In the meantime the Ryde and Newport Railway (R&NR) had been built and this was opened in 1875. The R&NR by the way was very unusual for a 'rural' railway as, in its early years, it only carried passengers.

In 1875 the C&NR and the R&NR formed a Joint Committee. In 1879 this took over the operation of the IW&NJR, and in 1887 all three companies amalgamated to form the Isle of Wight Central Railway (IWCR), a grand title for one of the poorest railways in Great Britain - poor in every sense.

The next railway to be opened was the much-needed line from Ryde Pier Head to make a junction at Ryde St John's Road with the terminus of the IWR and the IWCR. This railway was built jointly by the London Brighton & South Coast and the London & South Western Railway, the latter Company being responsible for the details of its construction. It replaced a tramway, the complexities of whose history are not for this article. This line was operated by the Joint Companies but the trains were provided by the IWR and the IWCR.

The next railway to be built was the Freshwater, Yarmouth & Newport (FYNR). This opened in 1889 and from then until 1913 it was operated by the IWCR. In 1913 the Freshwater Company fell out with the Central and decided to work the line itself, which it proceeded to do with some hastily acquired stock from the mainland and a number of carriages and wagons it was obliged to purchase from the IWCR.

The last railway to be built was the so-called Newport, Godshill and Ventnor Railway. This ran from its junction with the IWCR at Merstone, and was opened to St Lawrence in 1897 and to Ventnor in 1900. The whole point about this railway was to provide a better connection to Ventnor from the mainland via Southampton and Cowes. The Central operated it. Well, despite the high hopes of its promoters, it never paid its way and with the benefit of hindsight it should never have been built. One might say the same of most of the Island's railways but that is to forget the state of the Island's roads at the time: and, of course, at that time the railway was, the cutting edge of transport technology: although to use such a description for anything to do with the early years of the IWCR is a joke indeed. In fairness the Central was much improved in its later years and as for the IWR, that was for many years a well-run little railway but even that line never paid well enough to renew its rolling stock and had eventually to purchase second hand.

So what about the trains? Well, the IWR was well enough provided for in its early years. It had a fleet of very well-built Beyer Peacock 2-4-0Ts and new purpose-built carriages and wagons. Additional carriages required in later years came from the North London Railway and replacement stock for the original carriages from the Metropolitan Railway, the well-known non-bogie eight-wheelers.

The C&NR started life with two purpose-built 2-2-2Ts and three unusually long purpose-built carriages plus a few second-hand vehicles. The IW&NJR acquired three purpose-built carriages and a few second-hand vehicles but had to hire a locomotive. The R&NR had two new Beyer Peacock 2-4-0Ts much smaller than the IWR ones, and eleven second-hand carriages that had originated on the London & Birmingham Railway.

In due course the IWCR purchased a new and

A Waterloo - Portsmouth stopping service between Liphook and Liss: a 2 BIL is leading a later post-war 2 HAL. Alongside note the then standard SR power cable run with the control cable below. The conductor rails are on the cess side which was the standard position for the LSWR. In SR days it still amounted to about 60% of the position on double track line.

useful 4-4-0T and a modernised version of the R&NR 2-4-0T tanks. They also managed to purchase new a rail-motor, two bogie carriages and a number of wagons but everything else was second-hand although amongst these items it did manage to pick up four LB&SCR 'Terriers'. They were the mainstay of its not inconsiderable goods services and without doubt were the most useful engines it ever owned.   The FYN? Well, it made out with another second-hand 'Terrier' and a useful Manning Wardle 0-6-0ST. All the rolling stock was second-hand although seven carriages provided by the Great Central were found by the Southern to be amongst the best carriages on the Island. All in all a fascinating railway system but one the Southern found to be in need of almost complete renewal.

The Southern was not entirely taken by surprise because in 1921 a group of senior South Western officers, in expectation of having to take charge of the Island's railways sooner or later, went over to have a look. They were not impressed. The IWR was in the best condition, the track and bridges were in a fair state, the carriages were fit for a few years yet but the locomotive position was becoming critical; several of the engines were simply worn out. The Central was much worse. Again several of the engines were worn out as was virtually all the rolling stock. The track was poor and in some places the original. Worse still, some

of the bridges were also too lightly constructed to take more modern locomotives.

The Freshwater engines and some of the rolling stock were in quite good order but all the track needed renewing and the two viaducts would need strengthening if they were to take heavier locomotives.

And so it was that the SR was hardly five months old before the first two O2s arrived in LSWR livery, because that of the Southern had not yet been decided upon. There could be no argument as to what engines to send as there was nothing else remotely suitable, and happily they proved ideal. Over the years more O2s were sent over for use on the Ventnor line releasing the best of the IWR engines to go over to Newport. In the meantime first the Ryde to Cowes line bridges and track were upgraded and then the Newport to Sandown line. The Freshwater line was re-laid slowly but it was not until the two viaducts were strengthened in 1932 that the O2s were allowed to use it. The Ventnor West line kept the last of its original 67 lb FB rail until 1931 but that did not matter as this line was to be worked by 9-ton axle load push-pull fitted 'Terriers'.

Hand in hand with everything else went route and signalling improvements with new loops at Wroxall and Havenstreet, line doubling between Ryde St Johns and Smallbrook and again between Brading and Sandown.

Ryde Pier Head. Ryde St Johns Road and Newport station layouts were all rebuilt as were St Helens and Medina wharfs, elsewhere there were many other lesser improvements too numerous to mention.

The replacement of the carriage stock was a bit of a dog's breakfast to start with. A couple of ex-LC&DR 4-wheeled push-pull sets for the Ventnor West line were a good start as were three sets of elderly South Western bogie coaches, although two of them had to come from the Plymouth, Devonport and South West Junction Railway to whom they had been sold. They were for use on the old Central routes to Sandown and Ryde. Five sets of old Brighton four-wheelers were harder to explain. To make them up, some of the coaches had to come out of the "Lancing Belle"! They were used on the Bembridge and Freshwater lines. AB MacLeod told me that as an old Brighton man he was ashamed of them. Another mistake was the two sets of ex-SE&CR rail-motors intended for the Freshwater line but returned to the mainland a couple of years later. By 1928 it was decided to standardise on ex-LCDR four-wheeled vehicles. These were rather basic carriages but they were very well-built. In due course they were followed by their bogie counterparts. The Southern followed an almost continuous process of upgrading the carriage stock both to benefit the passengers and to keep down the work load on Ryde works. In due course Brighton bogie stock replaced the LC&DR four-wheelers and after the war ex-SE&CR bogie stock replaced the LC&DR bogies.

The goods stock was standardised on Brighton-designed vehicles, a few of which were actually brand new. For goods brake vans however, L&SWR "Road Vans" were selected. As is well known, all this stock was transferred on the deck of the SR's Southampton-based floating crane. It was a neat solution but an expensive one, the crane requiring the attention of up to four tugs. One wonders if a specially-built ferry barge might not have been a better idea.

Was all this work worthwhile? Undoubtedly it was. The passenger numbers increased year on year and whilst this of course ceased during the war, it continued to grow thereafter until I guess it peaked around 1955 or so. After that it declined rapidly under the influence of cheap overseas holidays and the arrival of motoring for all.

All this leads naturally to consider the electrification of the Portsmouth Direct line with which the fortunes of the Island in Southern days were so closely associated. However before any additional services could be brought into Waterloo, it was essential to increase the line capacity of the approach route and in particular to sort out the problems of the "main line" side of Waterloo itself.

As it was, the approach lines were laid out as Up Local, Up Through, Down Through, and Down Local. This made good sense further out, but meant that all Up suburban traffic had to cross the Up and Down Through lines in order to reach the main line side local platforms. The Windsor lines were not affected by this problem as they were virtually a separate railway. The answer was to build a flyover out at Wimbledon, the first place where there was room for it, so that now the lines became Up and Down Through and Up and Down Local, and to re-signal the lot with four-aspect colour-light signals out as far as Hampton Court Junction on the main line, and Clapham East on the Windsor side. New signal boxes were called for at Waterloo, Surbiton and Hampton Court Junction, plus very considerable alterations at those other boxes in the area that were retained.

The total amount of work for all departments was enormous and one can only marvel at the amount of planning, designing and construction involved: a new fly-over, a completely new permanent-way layout on the main line side at Waterloo and of course the signalling, but on the morning of 18 October 1936 the last train signalled by semaphores arrived at Waterloo at 12.35am and the first signalled by colour-light left at 1.30am. For everyone involved it was a tremendous achievement all carried out in less than two years.

This paved the way for the Portsmouth No. 1 scheme and later, via what the Southern was pleased to call the Mid-Sussex, the No. 2 scheme. The South Western does not seem to have realised the potential of their Portsmouth route but the Southern did. It was a difficult line to work in steam days and the D15s and later Schools may well have done their finest work on this route, but with its heavy grades and many curves it was a natural for electrification.

Use was again made of Government loans. The Portsmouth No. 1 scheme ran from Hampton Court Junction to Portsmouth Harbour and included Weybridge to Staines, Virginia Water to Guilford via Ascot and Aldershot and Woking to Alton. Power supply was again by remote-controlled sub-stations and "TP Huts" supervised by electrical Controls at Woking and Havant. The Weybridge to Staines line was commissioned on January 3 1937, Portsmouth and Farnham on April 11 1937 and to Alton on 4 of July.

The associated infrastructure work on both schemes was very heavy, with new stations at Surbiton, Woking, Havant and Horsham and extensive works at many other locations, including a new goods depot at Fratton to replace that at Portsmouth Town. There were new signal boxes at Surbiton, Woking, Dorking North, Arundel and Bognor. Car sheds were provided at Wimbledon Park, Farnham, Littlehampton and Fratton, all with washing machines. Two familiar features that made their appearance with these schemes were chain-link fencing and, I believe, the familiar bar and circle station name boards.

It was said that when electrification to Portsmouth was first being discussed consideration was given to going via the Meon Valley. Although this was a single line, provision had been made for doubling and it was a "modern", well-laid-out route. The only problems would seem to have been the severe curves at Fareham and between Cosham and Portcreek Junctions. One imagines

Seaton as seen from the top of the goods yard crane. The Southern completely rebuilt the station to take 10-coach trains which ran on Summer Saturdays to serve the adjacent holiday camp. The only portion of the original station to survive was the goods shed, very similar to the one at Colyton. Note how the goods yard roadway was flanked by a neat kerb finishing just clear of the sleeper ends.

this idea lasted just as long as it took to get to the ears of certain well-connected people in Haslemere. When I worked there in the late fifties this station had the greatest number of first-class season ticket holders on the Southern Region and that probably equated to the whole of Great Britain.

The No. 2 scheme took the juice from Dorking North to Havant, Three Bridges to Horsham, West Worthing to Ford Junction and included the Littlehampton and Bognor branches. These lines were commissioned on July 3rd 1938.

The local hunting fraternity were not best pleased by this development because, believe it or not, they had previously hunted across the tracks! Mind you the comment of the Southern's Chairman at the time, (Mr Robert Holland), took some beating. "Now, as to danger: the low voltage used (about 600) does not involve, in the case of a healthy person more than a sharp shock, there have therefore been few fatalities". Well, the later point was true but it was a foolish man who did not treat it with great care. If it did not kill you, a shorting arc could seriously burn or blind you.

I have wandered. Trains: the semi-fast services were provided for by the construction of further 2-BILs but for the fast services entirely new stock was built. These were 4-car units with a corridor connection at each end allowing free movement throughout the entire train.

There were three types: all had a 550HP (two 275 HP motors) motor brake third at each end. The 4 COR units had a compo and third in the middle, and there were eventually 54 of these. For use on the Portsmouth Direct there were 19 4 RES units. These had a Third Restaurant Car and a composite dining car. The two classes of dining facility were required because in the services officers and other ranks were not allowed to eat together and of course a large proportion of the passengers on this route were always RN personnel.

For the Mid-Sussex, 13 4-BUF units were supplied. These had a compo and third-class buffet car in the middle. The latter was heavily influenced by a certain Mr Bulleid then recently arrived at Waterloo. These buffet cars were painted a very vivid shade of green that was once described to me as yellow(!): and no, the man was a signalman and definitely not colour blind.

I have read that some considered these trains underpowered. If that were so it did not affect their ability to run very fast when asked to do so. I remember one Sunday evening when I was a box boy at Fratton West: A CRC (4-COR+4-RES+4-COR) had gone up to the Park as a Control-arranged special and I had given them its departure time. About an hour later Control rang back and asked for a time check. This was very unusual and I asked them what that was all about. Apparently this driver had got up there in something like 50 minutes which equated to an average speed of 75mph. The maximum speed? Only the driver knew that. We guessed he was on a finishing job!

On the question of livery, the Maunsell period used various shades of dark green with the commonly quoted lining of black and yellow. Now there is no doubt that in the early years that yellow was used, I have seen it for myself in good condition. However when a 4-COR motor coach turned up at Horsted Keynes a few years ago, it was seen to have orange lining. This was at once challenged but the Southern Electric Group was able to produce a SR instruction that clearly called for orange lining. My old friend in the Model Railway Club, the late Sid Dent, built very good 'O' gauge Southern models and he always used orange lining for his coaches and the paint came from Ashford works. What does one make of this? Well I think yellow was definitely the colour used until sometime in the early-to-mid thirties after which the colour was changed to orange. Incidentally we had a collection of photographs in the office taken at Portsmouth Harbour station in 1946 that showed that nearly all the 4-COR/RES units portrayed were still in their pre-war lined livery

I will round off this article with mention of Maunsell's later locomotives. The first to be considered are the W class 2-6-4Ts, Fifteen of these three-cylinder tanks were built between 1932-6 for working the cross-London freights; Nos. 1911-25. Their construction was long delayed and well spread by the downturn in freight traffic caused by the slump. As engines they might best be described as a tank version of the N1s. They incorporated the tanks, bunkers and bogies of the ill-fated 'Rivers' and were not allowed to work passenger trains but why this should be I do not know. In fact, trials with one on a passenger train did take place on the Oxted line in 1948 but the engine, fresh out of works, was found to ride badly at speed and that was the end of that. There can be no doubt that a Maunsell 2-6-4T did not ride well and Mr Ellison was more than justified in his reservations about them. For their intended duties however they were fine and they must have more than earned their keep over the years.

Then there was a final batch of fifteen 'Schools', Nos. 925-39, built between 1934-5. The Southern's passenger traffic held up quite well in this generally troubled period. The 'Schools' were followed by ten more of the equally fine Maunsell S15s. The construction of these engines was again heavily delayed and they were eventually built in 1936. The rebuilding of the Brighton 'Baltic' tanks into 4-6-0 tender engines must not be forgotten. It was hoped that these engines could take their place alongside the 'King Arthurs' on the Western Division but the South Western men could not get on with them and they eventually found a home at Basingstoke where they worked the Waterloo stoppers and the Reading-Portsmouth services. There must have been some good in them however, as during the war they were loaned to the GWR and I have read of a Great Western man who spoke very well of them, and knowing a few Western men that is praise indeed.

A batch of proposed locomotives that never got built were ten LB&SCR E2s. They would have been interesting engines, the money intended for them was eventually used to build the first three "oil-engined" 350HP shunters. It was not the done thing to speak of Diesels at the time.

Sadly we have to end the Maunsell story with another class that somehow never quite came up to expectations, the Qs. There were twenty of these, Nos. 530-49 built between 1938-9. They were supposed to replace the ageing Stirling O1s, the Billinton C2s and the Adams 0395s. They were nominally much more powerful and bigger than any of these classes but sadly they had no sparkle in them. Again, horses for courses perhaps, the Eastleigh men disliked them: to quote one " -a three set is all they want, son". On the other hand the Brighton men managed ten-coach Ramblers' Excursions with them.

Maunsell had remained in office until Sir Herbert Walker retired in 1937. In roughly fifteen years Sir Herbert had taken the Southern Railway from the subject of daily scorn and abuse to that of a first class main line railway, second to none in the land. It possessed the largest electrified suburban system in the world; the largest fleet of passenger ships in the country; and Southampton Docks, the nation's foremost passenger port. All this was achieved under the leadership of Sir Herbert Ashcombe Walker, KCB; a fine railwayman but above all else a very astute business man. Did he make any mistakes? Well, he was human and there must have been a few. The loss of the military train ferries, perhaps, and he did appoint a certain Mr Bulleid, from the LNER!

Main References-

Sir Herbert Walker's Southern Railway. C F Clapper.
Southern Electric 1909-1968. G T Moody
Southern Electric. David Brown .
The Isle of Wight Railway etc. R J M aycock & R Silsbury are the best.
Locomotives of the South Eastern & Chatham Railway. D L Bradley
The Southern Railway Magazine.

SOUTHERN SECRETS

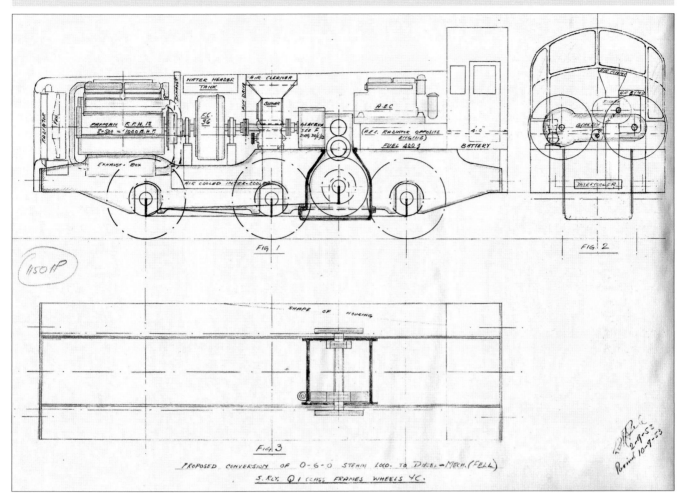

PROPOSED CONVERSION OF 0-6-0 STEAM LOCO. TO DIESEL-MECH. (FELL)
S. R.Y. Q1 CLASS FRAMES WHEELS &C.

Knowing our interest in the unusual, Mike Gipson kindly sent in this 1953 drawing as a result of digging around on the 'Fell' diesel locomotive. (The latter is a topic we would love to do some work on at later date although it is not really Southern orientated.) The above *is* though aimed directly at the Southern, a conversion using components from a 'Q1' to turn what was a steam locomotive into a jackshaft driven diesel machine intended as a light-passenger machine.

Sharp-eyed readers will of course notice a distinct family likeness to the Bulleid SR/BR-Paxman 0-6-0 diesel No 11001 from 1950. (Unfortunately dimensions, notably the wheelbase are not given on the drawing.)

Lt Col Fell had several diesel-mechanical designs prepared (in addition to his 4-8-4 [later converted to 4-4-4-4 type]) that operated on BR from 1952 to 1958. This 0-6-0 diesel shunter was destined to exist only on paper. But what is interesting on reading some of the technical detail is the connection that existed between Fell and Ricardo engineering from Shoreham. Remember Ricardo was also the firm that Bulleid had become involved with, reference sleeve-valves on 'Leader' only a few years earlier.

Conversions from steam? - not really as far fetched

as it might seem. After all the designer of GT3 J O P Hughes envisaged his locomotive type would see the re-use of the frames of redundant steam locomotives: the boiler / smokebox / firebox / cylinder assemblies being removed and substituted with a Gas Turbine power plant. Lt Col Fell saw the same potential but it appears, perhaps slightly earlier. (We have to be careful here as GT3 was in fact many years in gestation, so the design would have been fixed some time before it actually ran for the first time in 1961.) But our drawing distinctly states: "Proposed conversion of 0-6-0 steam loco to Diesel-Mechanical (Fell). Southern Railway Q1 Class frames, wheels etc."

It does not appear there was ever any successful large-scale conversion, or should we say 'interim' programme whereby steam components were re-used in alterative forms of motive power anywhere. Possibly this was because of costs whilst it was also easier to go straight to a newer form of traction starting from scratch. Even so it must be said that both 11001 and the Fell proposal show there was this option available. Yet again it seems the Southern could have shown the way.

With grateful thanks to Mike Gipson and The Paxman Archive.

AN EVENING OF STEAM AND DIESEL

Mike Green

For just over three hours on a spring evening, 4 April 1966, Mike Green was at Eastleigh recording arrivals and departures together with their associate workings. At a time when Southern steam had just over a year to survive there was still a healthy proportion of steam present even though this was by now restricted to 'Bulleid' pacifics and 'Standard' types. Representing 'modern' motive power were the SR's ubiquitous 'D65xx' locomotives, the existence of which had also allowed many older SR steam types to be withdrawn. Representing most local passenger workings were the 'Hampshire' DEMU sets. Not a single electric train was seen, but then that was not surprising as the 3rd rail was not energised through Eastleigh until the end of 1966.

Time	LOCOMOTIVE No.	Cl.	Name	STOCK Vans	Coaches	Notes	WORKING	PLT/ ROAD	COMMENTS UT=Up through. DT= Down through
6.37	1132				3	DEMU	P&S'sea to Romsey	1	
6.38	73119	5MT	Elaine	1	11		Semi-fast to Wat'loo	2	
6.44	1121				2	DEMU	So'ton Ter to Reading	2	
6.48	1127				3	DEMU	ECS from So'ton Term.	2	Shunted to Platform 4
6.50	73016	5MT				Light Engine	From shed to platform	4	See note 1
6.57	1127				3	DEMU ex Platform 2	In front of 73016	4	See below
6.58	D6540	15/6		4		BV + 3 vans	Ex Western Docks	UT	
6.58	34005	WC	Barnstaple		10		5.22 ex Waterloo	DT	
7.00	76069	4MT				Light Engine	Ex shed to yard	UT	See below
7.02	1107				3	DEMU	Alton to So'ton Term.	3	
7.03	1122				2	DEMU	So'ton Term. to Alton	2	
7.15	76061	4MT			6		5.40 B'mouth to Wat'loo	1	
7.19	35022	MN	Holland America Line	1	10	Boat Train ECS	Ex So'ton Docks	UT	
7.20	76069	4MT		34		1 BV & 33 wagons & vans	Ex yard (3.16 ex Felt.)	DT	Inc 20 cement wagons
7.21	1127				3	DEMU	E'leigh to So'ton Ctl.	4	Departure time
7.26	34095	WC	Brentor		13		Semi-fast to B'mouth	3	
7.31	D6506	15/6		28		1 BV & 27 wagons & vans	Ex Western Docks	2	To Yard
7.33	1133				3	DEMU	Reading to So'ton Term.	3	
734	1128				3	DEMU	P&S to Romsey	1	
7.37	73016	4MT			3	Departure time	Slow to Southampton	4	See 6.50 arrival & Note 1
7.39	1132				3	DEMU	Romsey to Eastleigh	4	
7.41	75079	4MT		50		1 Bogie BV & 49 mixed	Ex Western Docks	UT	
7.43	D6506	15/6				Light Engine	Ex Yard to Shed	3	See below
7.44	1103/7				6	2 x DEMU split at Platform	1107 So'ton to Reading	2	See below for 1103
7.48	34026	WC	Yes Tor		10		6.14 from Waterloo	DT	Extra
7.49	34002	WC	Salisbury		11	Original form	5.30 from Weymouth	UT	
7.53	1103				3	DEMU ex Platform 2 at 7.51		4	See below
7.54	D6515	15/6		31		1 BV & 30 mixed	To Feltham	UT	
7.58	34090	WC	Sir Eustace Missenden		3		Bas'stoke to So'ton Term.	3	Stopper See below
7.58	80065	4MT		14			Ex So'ton Term.	UT	
8.00	73110	5MT	The Red Knight		9		6.22 ex Waterloo	DT	
8.02	34090	BB	Sir Eustace Missenden	3		Departure time	Ex Basingstoke	3	See above
8.06	D6530	15/6		6			7.15 ex Salisbury	3	

Off the end of what was then Platform 3 at Eastleigh (in more recent time Platform 2), No 34031 'Torrington' carries the headcode for a Waterloo - Southampton Terminus stopping service but which was in fact a special troop-train working. 19 July 1959.

Tony Molyneaux / Noodle Books collection

8.06	D6530	15/6		6			7.15 ex Salisbury	3	
8.08	D6532	15/6		22		See note 2	Fawley to Eastleigh	UT	
8.11	1103			3		DEMU	Eastleigh to P&S	4	Departure time
8.12	35028	MN	*Clan Line*	12			6.30 ex Waterloo	DT	
8.13				3		DEMU	So'ton Term. to Reading	2	
8.15	75075	4MT				Van train	P&S to Eastleigh	1	
8.16	73171	5MT				Light Engine	Ex Shed to yard	UT	
8.24	1123			3		DEMU	to So'ton Term.	4	See note 3.
8.30	1109			3		DEMU	to So'ton Term.	4	See note 3
8.32	73080	5MT	*Merlin*	6			Semi-fast to Wat'loo	2	
8.37				3		DEMU	P&S to Romsey	1	
8.38	1122			2		DEMU	Alton to So'ton Term.	3	
8.41	D6545	15/6				Light Engine	Ex Shed to yard	UT	
8.44	D6532	15/6				Light Engine	Ex Yard to Shed	2	
8.53	D6585	15/6				Light Engine	Ex Shed to Yard	UT	
8.56	1123			3		DEMU	So'ton Term to R'ing	2	

9.02	73086	5MT	*The Green Knight*	1	9			7.24 ex Waterloo	DT	Extra
9.03	1105				3	DEMU		Salisbury to P&S	4	
9.05	80151	4MT		16					2	Shunt back into Yard
9.06	D6528	15/6				Light Engine		Ex Shed to Yard	UT	
9.10	75078	4MT		8				Left vans in platform	1	See below
9.15					2	DEMU		To So'ton Cental	3	
9.15	D6514	15/6		27		See note 4		Ex Fawley	UT	
9.22	D6528	15/6		33		1 BV & 33 mixed		Ex Yard	DT	
9.26					3	DEMU		Romsey to Eastleigh	4	
9.27	1122				2	DEMU		So'ton T to Eastleigh	2	
9.28	73169	5MT				Light Engine		Ex Yard to shed	DT	
9.29	1122				2	DEMU		ECS to yard	2	
9.32	D6541	15/6				Light Engine		Ex Shed. To Yard?	UT	
9.32	35013	MN	*Blue Funnel*	1	10			7.30 ex Waterloo	3	Arrival time. See below
9.34	D6506	15/6				Light Engine		Ex shed	UT	Backed onto vans later
9.36	D6523	15/6				Light Engine		Ex Shed. To yard?	UT	
9.37	D6506	15/6				Light Engine		Attached to vans	1	Reversed from UT
9.40	34082	BB	*615 Squadron*	9	5			Semi-fast to Wat'loo	2	Arrival time. See below
9.45	35013	MN	*Blue Funnel*	1	10			7.30 ex Waterloo	3	Departure time
9.46	34082	BB	*615 Squadron*	9	5			Semi-fast to Wat'loo	2	Departure time

No 73029 in smart clean green livery waiting at the London end of the up main platform at Eastleigh (then Platform 2 but more recently Platform 1) sometime in 1963.

Rev. D Littlefair

Note 1: 73016 arrived in Platform 4 prior to 6.35. It proceeded to the shed, tender first, leaving the coaches in the platform. It returned at 6.50 having turned and re-coupled up to them. The train then left at 7.37 as a stopping train to Southampton Central where it waited and followed the 6.30 from Waterloo as a stopping train to Bournemouth.

Note 2: The train consist included 18 tank wagons from Fawley and three vehicles from the MOD at Marchwood.

Note 3: One of these two trains is from Alton the other from Reading but I only noted them as shown. 1123 returned later as a train to Reading. On the basis of what happened with 1107 in that it came from Alton and went to Reading, then 1123 would have been the train from Alton with 1109 being the delayed Reading train.

Note 4: The train consist was Bogie Brake Van + 2 wagons + 22 Tank Wagons + 1 Van + Brake Van.

Note 5: The Class reference 15/6 is an amendment to 15/1 given to the D65xx series by the Eastern Region in the early 1960s under the reference 'Eastern Region Diesel Classification'. This covered all diesel types and not just those working on the ER.

Note 6: It would appear that only the last two semi-fasts dwelt any length of time in the station. Could this have been to deal with post office traffic?

Opposite *- Steam (No 35017 'Belgian Marine' and an unidentified DEMU set on the down lines at Eastleigh, 19 July 1959. The brick building nearest the camera was used by diesel men working the DEMU sets.*

Tony Molyneaux / Noodle Books collection

Were you a trainspotter? From a personal perspective that would depend entirely on definition. If within the definition of liking trains - specific type / age / origin / area - then yes. If in the literal sense of liking everything to do with railways, then a definite no. Similarly does the word include someone who watched but did not record numbers, somehow I never got around to that but again thousands did.

From the 1950s probably through to the early/mid 1960s were the zenith for the trainspotter, ably assisted of course by the Ian Allan spotters-books and the associated 'Locospotters Club' - remember the badges in their respective regional colours…..? Allied to this were the enthusiast groups accessible to a more select audience. 'O.U.R.S.' for the Oxford University Railway Society with a similar venture at Cambridge. (Folklore has it that on one day a year each would take over a local branch line and be responsible for almost everything for that day. Under supervision of course!)

For other mortals there were the special trains, again initially Ian Allan Excursions, often taking enthusiasts on works / shed visits and so making accessible locations where public access was invariably prohibited. (Locally some sheds and depots were easy to access others not so - relying upon knowledge passed on by word-of-mouth between groups of enthusiasts.) Sadly there were also always one or two who would ruin it for majority.

With the proliferation of line closures and engine type withdrawals from the late 1950s onwards so special workings

Above and opposite pages. Waterloo with No 35018 attracting a gathering of enthusiasts (the school uniform style of attire as applied to most from the period is always worthy of a second glance.) The next generation would pay as much attention to the 'COR' set alongside. Promiment also is the Waterloo Station master with the headgear as befits his office.

saw crowds of enthusiasts on long trains travelling over a line where normally just a single coach alone might be seen. This also brought strange engines to unusual routes as witness the visits by various Bulleid Pacifics to the Midlands and North in the mid-1960s as well as various Eastern Region types on to Southern metals.

John Bird in his superlative 'Southern Steam Sunset/Surrender' volumes gives detail of some of these specials of the later years of steam but it should not be forgotten that as times (and tastes) have changed so more modern traction once despised as ousting steam or older electric traction, has itself developed a following all of its own.

One final story may perhaps be recounted as recalled by Colin Judge, one of the founders of the original 'OPC' publishing venture. Colin comments that in the 1970s it was still possible to arrange for a train to traverse a line which might not have seen any form of service for some years. The actual occasion was in the Welsh Valleys and where, after much negotiation, it had been arranged for a 11-coach special to visit the end of a branch, the last previous train of any type being almost two decades before. BR, it seemed, only too willing to assist, OPC saw the opportunity where they would (and indeed did) have a captive audience for their books. A few days before, an inspection of the infrastructure pronounced it suitable - subject to a restricted speed limit of course, whilst at the same time various items of debris (old cars, bicycles and supermarket -trolleys) were removed from the 'four-foot'.

Come the day and the train duly traversed the route, welcomed by cheering locals delighted to see their railway in use again. Everyone was joyous and had truly entered into the spirit of the occasion, well almost everyone, the exception a solitary man whose privy door faced on to the railway and who over the years had left the door open content in the knowledge there would never be a train that might pass during his 'ablutions'. Well it was all his own fault that he chose to use his facilities just at that moment….. .

(A special exhibition on the era of 'Trainspotting' is scheduled to take place at the National Railway Museum from September 2014 to Spring 2015.)

Opposite and above - *Slightly earlier in time on 2 February 1947 was this event involving No 21C16 - Ian Allan is standing in the raincoat with his back to the cab in the above view. Clearly this was something the newsreels / BBC were also recording, although the group of cameramen are clearly less than enamoured with the occasion!*   *All views - courtesy Ian Allan*

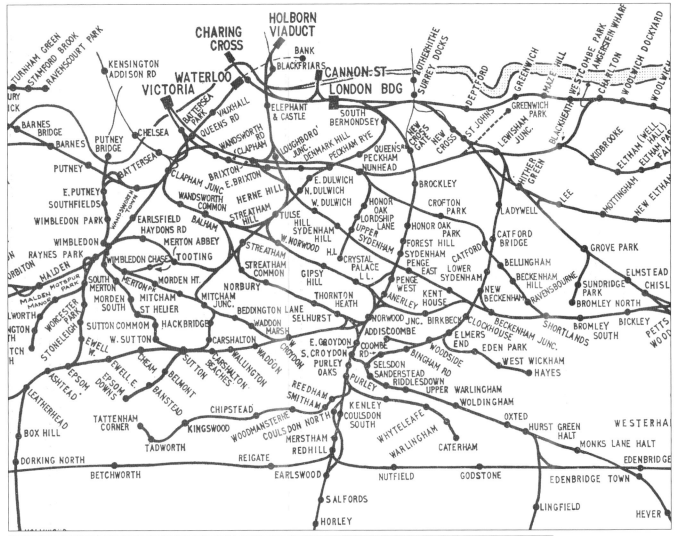

'UI' class 2-6-0 No 31900 comes off the West London Extension line at Clapham Junction heading a train of Midland stock. The No 25 headcode as applied here 'LMR via West London Line', gives no clue as to the train's ultimate destination though it is likely to be a South Coast resort.

The Lens of Sutton Association.

The West End of London & Crystal Palace Railway

Jeremy Clarke

The London & Croydon Railway opened between [West] Croydon and Corbetts Lane Junction on 5th June 1839 with running powers thence over the London & Greenwich Railway into its own London Bridge station, north of the Greenwich one. The London & Brighton Railway had use of both the London & Croydon and the London & Greenwich on the completion of its line from Brighton Junction (Norwood) to Haywards Heath on 12 July 1841 and the South Eastern joined the party from 26 May 1842 from the opening of the first stage of its Dover line between Reigate Junction [Redhill] and Tonbridge.

Four years later, on 27 July 1846, an Amalgamation Act for the London & Croydon and the London & Brighton to form, with others, the London, Brighton & South Coast Railway received Parliamentary assent. Expansion of the Brighton system really began from that point. Earlier that year the L&BR had been authorised to make a line from Croydon to Wandsworth via Streatham with the intent of continuing into the London & South Western's Nine Elms terminus. This was a response to the newly-established joint ownership at Portsmouth following sanction of the LSWR line from Fareham to Portcreek Junction, (opened throughout 1/10/48). Construction of the L&B line had not been started when Waterloo superseded Nine Elms as the LSWR's London terminus in July 1848. At that time William Chaplin, the South Western's chairman, may have been alluding to this route when he stated encouragingly that the four lines laid into the new terminus would provide sufficient paths for other companies' trains without delaying those of his own.

But not all such expansion was made in the name of the LBSCR itself. The authorised line to Wandsworth was eventually constructed but not before another initially independent one had got the company into the capital's 'West End'. The Great Exhibition of 1851 had been housed at Hyde Park in the splendid iron and glass greenhouse designed by Joseph Paxton for which a contributor to 'Punch' magazine coined the title 'The Crystal Palace', even before the building had been approved. At the conclusion of the exhibition, which had been limited in duration to six months, the future of this masterpiece was uncertain. Despite some opposition a business consortium was put together to form a company intent on rebuilding the structure on another site.

Besides Paxton himself and other prominent businessmen, the London, Brighton & South Coast Railway had a strong representation within this consortium in the form of Samuel Laing, the Brighton's Chairman, and Leo Schuster, a member of the Brighton Board. He not only followed Laing into the LBSCR Chair but owned the 280 acres of Penge Place and its substantial park, once part of Penge Common. This was located on the rise to and at the top of Sydenham Hill which, with a maximum height of about 350′ above sea level, provides spectacular views over

Stroudley 'D' class 0-4-2T No 271 'Eridge', departs from the Brighton's 'down local' platform at Clapham junction about the turn of the 20th century. The headcode is No 39 which covers the Victoria-Portsmouth route via Mitcham Junction, Epsom, Horsham and the Mid-Sussex line, though it is likely the train will terminate no further south than Dorking.
The Lens of Sutton Association.

The Beckenham Junction push/pull set consisting of two Billinton coaches, 'fore-and-aft', the unidentified tank engine - probably a Stroudley 'D1' 0-4-2T - stands in the bay at Crystal Palace early in the 20th century.

The Lens of Sutton Association

much of south and south-east London. Schuster was persuaded to sell this property to the Palace consortium which began re-erecting the building there in August 1852.

The finished article, re-opened by Queen Victoria, was built on a rather larger footprint than the original with additional transepts as well as a different roof profile, and had been set on the highest part of the park which thus fell away from it toward the east. It is safe to assume that Laing in particular had looked some way beyond merely re-erecting the Palace at Penge, for the eastern fringe of the park lay only yards from the main London-Brighton railway line. Even as reconstruction began the LBSCR put a bill before Parliament seeking authority for a double-track, mile-long branch line starting at a junction just south of Sydenham to a new and palatial station located on the southern border of the park. These opened on 10 June 1854, contemporaneously with the Palace.

The down branch line, which is ten chains longer than the up one, crossed the main line formation – soon to be four tracks wide - on a flyover, its principal purpose being to ease the upward gradient to the new station rather than eliminate flat junctions. Sydenham's down side platform had to be moved to the north side of the bridge carrying Sydenham Road over the railway to make room for the divergence. This resulted in a 'staggered platform'

layout until 1982 when the up platform had also to be moved north due to the deterioration and threatened collapse of the retaining wall behind it.

The original layout at the Crystal Palace station was of four dead-end platform lines but set between six platform faces to assist swift passenger movement, all under cover of a bow-spring arch roof. (This was dismantled following the collapse, with some loss of life, of a similar structure at Charing Cross station in December 1905. The centre supporting wall was demolished at the same time.)

On the heels of Parliamentary approval for the Sydenham-Crystal Palace branch, a West End of London & Crystal Palace Railway received authorisation in 1853. This company proposed to build a line from the LSWR at Wandsworth to make an end-on junction at Crystal Palace with this new branch from Sydenham. Once more the intention was for this line to continue from Wandsworth into Waterloo. But the South Western's enthusiasm for this arrangement later waned and, arguing that Waterloo could not after all accommodate WEL&CPR traffic, it withdrew from the contract negotiations in 1855.

The LBSCR supported this new Crystal Palace–Wandsworth line, by word if not perhaps by deed or finance, and agreed to work it, mainly because it went some way towards meeting its perceived need to gain a terminal in the

West End, the L&BR proposal of the previous decade having fallen by the wayside, for the time being at least. The major work on the new line, the 746 yard-long tunnel beneath Sydenham Hill, proved difficult to construct because of the unstable nature of the clay. The tunnel also passed directly beneath one of the two massive water towers providing a 'head' to the fountains in the park. A contemporary report states the work *'.... taxed in its execution all the skill and workmanship of the eminent contractors'*. Nevertheless, the line opened on 1 December 1856 to a temporary terminus at Wandsworth Common, a distance of four-and-a-half-miles. This station lasted only until March 1858, closing upon the opening of New Wandsworth, only a half-mile shy of the present Clapham Junction.

Less than a year after commissioning of the WEL&CPR another important connection had been made with the Brighton main line from London Bridge. From a junction almost in the tunnel mouth at Crystal Palace, the station now having had two terminal lines converted into 'through' ones, another branch just under 1½ miles long passed to the south of the original building to make south-facing connections some 20 chains north of Norwood Junction. It opened on 1 October 1857. Seven months later, under the cumbersome title 'West End of London & Crystal Palace Railway (Farnborough Extension)', this line had gone eastward from Bromley Junction to Shortlands, (then titled Bromley).

The Mid-Kent Railway opened to Beckenham Junction from Lewisham on 1 January 1857 and eighteen months later it had extended from Shortlands to Southborough Road (Bickley). There it awaited the oncoming London, Chatham & Dover Railway line from Rochester, the two meeting on 3 December 1860. By use of the Farnborough Extension the LCDR gained an access route to London though its trains were not permitted to call at any WEL&CPR station beyond Crystal Palace. The Brighton had leased the WEL&CPR in 1858 but did not work the Farnborough Extension. Instead, the West End company itself operated a shuttle between Crystal Palace and Beckenham Junction until it was purchased by the LBSCR in 1859.

Meanwhile, with the South Western out of the equation, further extension of the WEL&CPR took the line to Thames-side close to Battersea Pier on 29 March 1858. That year saw another independent enter the picture with the sanctioning of the Victoria Station & Pimlico Railway. This was authorised to make a junction with the WEL&CPR close to its terminus at Battersea pier and build a bridge across the Thames to a new station *'near Victoria Street, Pimlico'*.

From the laying of the foundation stone exactly one year elapsed before the first engine crossed Grosvenor Bridge, on 9 June 1860. However, the Board of Trade at first refused to sanction use of the bridge for general traffic, which delayed its opening until 1 October 1860. (The original WEL&CPR terminal station at Battersea Pier was actually named Pimlico.) That year also saw the section of

Wandsworth Common looking south. Despite the nearby New Wandsworth yard the sidings are packed with wagons for the local coal merchants. The nearest gas lamp has a '6-car' stop marker on the glass while the distant signal at the end of the platform still retains a red arm in addition to the Coligny-Welch indicator by the spectacle plate

The Lens of Sutton Association

Longhedge Junction signalbox sits in the centre of the routes once owned by three different companies. The two tracks curving away to the left are ex-LBSCR from Ludgate Junction to Factory Junction, the pair immediately in front of the box are those of the West London Joint Railway from Latchmere Junction to Stewarts Lane and Grosvenor Bridge while the pair behind the box form the original WEL&CPR route to Battersea Pier/Pimlico. Transport Treasury / A E Bennett. 12 August 1956.

the West End company's line east of Bromley Junction being purchased by the Chatham.

The Brighton, having subscribed to half the VS&PR company's capital, was entitled to one half of Victoria station, the other half being leased jointly by the Chatham and the GWR from the opening of that part on 25 August 1862. In the interim LCDR trains had had use of the Brighton's facilities. The Chatham eventually opened its independent line clear of the WEL&CPR's curves and gradients so unwelcome to fast running on 1 July 1863. The Brighton itself had similarly shortened its route between Croydon and London by about a mile on opening the Windmill Bridge Junction to Balham line on 1 December 1862, roughly the route originally proposed by the L&B in 1846. More importantly, although this line was not free from gradients it was in the main a much easier proposition than the former WEL&CPR which, from that time, generally carried only local traffic.

The awkward curvature of the Victoria line through Stewarts Lane and sharp gradients from the point of passing under the LSWR main line out of Waterloo to the south end of Grosvenor Bridge caused the LBSCR to look for means of improving the working here. The outcome was a high level route from Pouparts Junction, some fifty chains beyond Clapham Junction, rising on a brick viaduct south of the original formation at a steady and curving 1 in 120 to the level of the Grosvenor bridge. *En route* it passed over both

its original line to Battersea and the South Western route out of Waterloo. The line opened on 1 May 1867, the Brighton providing a new station at Battersea Park, 1¼ miles from Victoria, at the same time. The South London Line, which made a junction immediately north of this station, was also provided with platforms here.

Shortly after this the Company began construction of a new locomotive depot in the shadow of the viaduct. Because of the restricted site the roundhouse-type was chosen, the first one being erected on the west – up - side of the viaduct by 1869. Eventually there were three of these, two on the up side with 55' diameter turntables, one with a 45-footer on the down side. Construction permitted closure of the small three-road shed that had been in place since the WEL&CPR's arrival at Battersea. The depot was accessible directly from the low-level lines at Stewarts Lane and by a spur from the up direction Victoria line. Not surprisingly the new depot adopted the Battersea name, its allocation carrying a plain 'B' shedcode on the platform angle-iron immediately behind the buffer-beam. Tank engines for local work formed the bulk of the allocation though some main line locomotives featured. (New Cross was for years deemed to be the Brighton's principal London depot.)

Electrification of Brighton lines from the early years of the 20th century, and especially once the third rail began to spread, saw Battersea's allocation steadily decline. With the modernisation of the former LCDR Stewarts Lane

Wandsworth Common looking north. The train arriving at the down local platform is drawn by a Billinton 'radial' tank in Marsh umber livery. The No 14 headcode applies to the Victoria - London Bridge route via Selhurst and Norwood Junction. This was lost in 1983 with the simplification and resignalling of the junctions at Gloucester Road north of Croydon.

Balham looking eastwards towards the junctions of the Crystal Palace and East Croydon lines. The date is 21 September 1952 shortly before semaphores gave way to power signalling.

Both the Lens of Sutton Association

depot in 1933, Battersea's days were numbered, the remaining engines and staff being transferred and the shed closing the following year though the buildings were still in place and use for many years afterwards, latterly as a lorry maintenance shop or as part of a coach park.

Further connections opened new routeing possibilities for the WEL&CPR with the completion of the line between Peckham Rye and Sutton on 1 October 1868 though advantage was not immediately taken of them. New spurs were opened between this line at Tulse Hill and West Norwood Junction on 1 November 1870, and taking the opposite direction, from Tulse Hill to Leigham Junction, eight months later.

The Chatham had already made a further connection with the Brighton by opening the three-quarter mile-long line between Herne Hill and Tulse Hill on 1st January 1869. In sum these connections improved and simplified the movement of 'through' traffic, particularly

freight. Their importance grew following the start of wagon sorting at Norwood Junction from the late 1870s and the establishment of sorting sidings by the LCDR itself at Herne Hill, with direct access thence to railway companies north of the Thames via Snow Hill and the Widened Lines. The major Brighton goods depots at Willow Walk and Battersea were similarly now easy of access.

The High-Level route into Victoria had been built three tracks wide, one down and two up, one for local and the other for distance traffic. Powers were obtained in August 1890 to add an additional down line for local trains. This was in place by 1894 although at the Battersea end some slewing of existing track saw the up main being provided with a new track instead. To this day, that line has never had a platform alongside it at Battersea Park and the viaduct over the South Western route is of a quite different design to the original.

Overhead electrification between Battersea Park

The down end of Crystal Palace shows the line to Beckenham Junction curving away to the left while coaches are berthed in sidings in the original part of the station to the right. One of Norwood's army of 'C2X' class 0-6-0 freight engines, No 32447, shunts the goods yard, quite properly displaying headcode No 10, 'Victoria or Battersea yard to Norwood Junction yard via Crystal Palace'. A down train is signalled. *Transport Treasury / R C Riley 12 March 1954.*

and Crystal Palace at 6700v AC came into use on 12 May 1911, the section over the bridge from Victoria having been wired as part of the South London Line installation eighteen months previously. The wires were extended from Crystal Palace through Norwood Junction to new car sheds and workshops at Selhurst a year later. As electrification applied only to local traffic this saw a change of use of the four lines between Victoria and Balham. Up to that time the tracks had been paired by direction but now were paired by description, 'Main' and 'Local'. Third rail electrification over the route began on 3 March 1929 and included the ex-LCDR non-electrified segment east of Bromley Junction, which had been closed in 1915 as a wartime economy measure. The branch from Sydenham to Crystal Palace had been equipped with the third rail the previous year. That was part of the new electrification scheme between Charing Cross/London Bridge and Coulsdon North/Purley and the former SER branches to Caterham and Tadworth.

The journey over the West End of London &

Crystal Palace Railway effectively begins nowadays at Norwood North Junction, a quarter-mile north of the station, where the spurs leave or gain the main line to/from London Bridge. Unlike any other part of the Brighton line the four tracks here are paired by direction with the 'fast' lines in the centre of the formation. Thus it is easy for the spurs off the 'slow' lines to make connections with the line to Beckenham at Bromley Junction.

The four tracks of the Brighton line are bridged before the down spur, twenty-seven chains long, bears away at 9 miles 41 chains from Victoria. The up spur is thirty-four chains long and meets the line from Beckenham Junction at 9 miles 36 chains from Victoria.

From heading north-westwards at Bromley Junction the line curves gradually toward the north, climbing on an embankment at 1 in 95/106 – catch points once being handily placed on the steeper gradient – and in the course of this, passing South Norwood Lake on the up side. This was one of two reservoirs serving the Croydon

'W' class 2-6-4T No 31921 (73A) approaches West Norwood Junction running light towards Crystal Palace. The four-arch bridge in the background was demolished by explosives on 14 June 1958 to permit road widening.

Transport Treasury / R C Riley 11 March 1954

Canal which the London & Croydon Railway purchased on 21 July 1836 to form the basis for its line. With its high dam right alongside the railway, the lake is now used purely for pleasure with fishing and boating both being available while at the same time supporting much wildlife, particularly waterfowl.

Having passed under Anerley Road the line swings sharply back toward the north-west and reaches Crystal Palace station (8m 56ch). This part is rather mean when compared to the original, being simply open platforms with a brick shelter on the down side and completely lacking any of its grandeur. Two down side bays once existed for use by the LCDR and LBSCR jointly-worked shuttle services to Beckenham Junction introduced in 1863, though these were withdrawn in 1917. One of the bay lines lay between two platforms while the other had a release loop. These later became berthing sidings.

A small goods yard having a short headshunt occupied the 'V' between the converging lines. With an outlet on to the down Beckenham line, it consisted of three roads, the goods shed spanning the siding closest to the bay

runround. The yard closed on 9 December 1965.

Three signalboxes governed movements around the station. East box, a survivor from earliest days of the Brighton 'eaveless' design, stood on the south side of the incoming spur from Sydenham while South box was on the down side of the line to Norwood, adjacent to the points into the goods yard. Tunnel box, as its name suggests, lay in a tight and very gloomy position between the tunnel mouth and the substantial buttress to the centre pier to the bridge forming the station's approach road, and in the centre of the converging tracks. In BR days these boxes became, respectively, 'C', 'B' and 'A'. 'B' box closed on 15 January 1967 and the other two on 13 July 1969. The station and, indeed, the line as a whole now comes under the Victoria Control Centre at Clapham Junction.

Like Norwood Junction, Crystal Palace is now in the hands of London Overground, trains from north of the Thames via Sydenham terminating here. The suitably impressive building dates from a comprehensive reconstruction in 1875 and stands just south of the line on the east side of the approach road which, at the north end,

A typical '6PUL/6PAN' formation at Wandsworth Common with a Victoria - Littlehampton working routed via Quarry and Worthing.   *Transport Treasury / R C Riley 5 August 1956.*

leads on into the park. A new ticket hall, whose arched glazed profile to a degree reflected the Crystal Palace, was opened in the 1980s but demolished as part of a major reconstruction undertaken by Transport for London in the autumn of 2012. Further refurbishment works, including improvements to the Victorian ticket hall as part of the takeover by TfL, were completed in March 2013. These improvements included the installation of lifts to provide full accessibility.

The junction between the two lines is right in the mouth of the tunnel at 8 miles and 47 chains from Victoria. The tunnel itself falls at 1 in 391, the line emerging into a cutting as it approaches Gipsy Hill where the gradient has steepened to 1 in 103. This station lies about halfway down the west side of the ridge formed by Sydenham Hill, the eponymous and steeply graded road bridging the line at the down end. The station building stands on the bridge, a pleasant single-storey structure with gabled roofs in the ends of which LBSCR crests have been inset facing the road. It underwent refurbishment in the early 1990s and again in 2009. Steps lead from the booking hall directly down to the platforms.

The goods yard consisted of three long roads,

though the one closest to and parallel with the up line may also have been used as a refuge siding. Its down end finished at a dock behind the up platform. No goods shed stood here though records show the yard had a 5-ton crane. Freight facilities were withdrawn on 7 October 1968. The signalbox, which opened in 1881, was on the down side by trailing points into another refuge siding. It closed on 13th July 1969.

Still falling, but much more steeply now as it descends into the valley of the River Effra, the line reaches West Norwood, just over seven miles from Victoria. The station is set partly in cutting and partly on the ten arches of the viaduct over the Effra, which has long been culverted underground. The river is formed from several streams rising on and below the western side of the Crystal Palace ridge that join and flow north to the Thames at Vauxhall. But from the point of crossing the South Circular Road in Dulwich it became in the mid-19th century part of the Southern High Level Sewer under Joseph Bazalgette's London sewerage system. Plans to uncover the upper reaches of the waterway have been voiced on a number of occasions in recent years.

The location below Sydenham Hill saw the area

Bulleid 'Light Pacific', No 34101 'Hartland', heads a special along the ex-LBSCR Norwood Spur between Birkbeck and Norwood Junction. Once double track, this line was singled in 1928 and thereafter only carried trains in the southbound direction. It was occasionally used for freight traffic, but very rarely indeed by any passenger service.

The Lens of Sutton Association

named Lower Norwood – Crystal Palace is, strictly speaking, a misnomer: it is actually in Upper Norwood – but the incomers who arrived here with the advance of new property development objected to living anywhere 'Lower'. This resulted in the change of prefix to 'West' in 1885, the station following suit on 1 January 1886. The station building faces Knights Hill, which bridges the line at the up end, the track dipping sharply beneath it, down at 1 in 69 and then up at 1 in 72. Norwood High Street passes beneath the railway about halfway along the platforms and forms the point at which the incoming curve of 17-chain radius reverses to one of 43-chains.

The station building was renewed in 1891 though CLASP structures superseded it and the platform buildings in 1969. There was no goods yard here, the local topography lacking any near level site for one. The signal

box was located high above the up platform, almost adjacent to the station building, but moved to the up platform in 1892, closing in March 1928 with its responsibilities passing to West Norwood Junction box.

On a gentle downgrade now, the line continues to turn more toward the north, latterly on a 21-chain curve, until it approaches the first of the connections with the Peckham Rye-Sutton line south of Tulse Hill. West Norwood Junction is almost 6¾ miles from Victoria, the double-track spur to Tulse Hill leaving on the down side. The signal box, of a type suggesting a wartime replacement of the original, was on that side also, right by the junction which is almost beneath an unusually-shaped bridge carrying a road junction. Incidentally, the four separate arches of the next road bridge were demolished by explosives on 14 June 1958. It had proved too narrow for

Streatham Hill station facing south showing the neat Brighton building on the bridge in the background and the up bay on the right. Note the wartime paintwork on the barley-twist standard of the nearest gas lamp.

The Lens of Sutton Association

the increasing road traffic of the area.

The line now bears sharply round towards the west, both up and down lines being check-railed until Leigham Junction where the double-track spur from Tulse Hill trails in at 6m 31ch. (The bridge over the line to Sutton is eight chains before this.) The box here, a small timber structure on a locking room appearing to have been reinforced for wartime by a substantial brick covering, opened in 1871 and was on the down side. Like its companion at West Norwood Junction it closed on 13 April 1969.

Still running downhill, but rather more quickly now as the line descends into the Thames valley, the route passes through the 443 yards of Leigham tunnel before, still in cutting, coming to Streatham Hill, (5m 57ch). This is the northernmost of the three ex-LBSCR stations in the locality, the timber building being on the west side of the bridge carrying the main A23 London-Brighton road over the track at the down end. Staircases lead out directly down to the platforms though lifts were installed as part of general improvement in 2009. The station was opened as Streatham & Brixton Hill though the end-on road junction with the latter is more than a half-mile to the north. The present name was settled on in 1869.

A west-facing bay platform on the up side was in regular use for starting rush-hour services until about 1960.

A signalbox was opened by the bay line's junction with the up line in 1898: it closed on 19 November 1967. The bay line is still in place but now classified 'up siding east' as part of the extensive carriage berthing and inspection facility alongside the up line. It extends the length of this facility as 'up siding west', a signalbox on the south side of the line governing the pointwork where the original outlet from the complex left the siding. A ground frame now exists on the same site.

Development of these berthing sidings began in the last few years of the 19th century with a rapid increase in facilities for the extended electrification scheme of June 1912, by which time nine roads of various lengths were available. These sidings had the advantage of being directly accessible from both London Bridge and Victoria stations. There are now eight sidings, all under cover though in two separate sheds - one twelve, the other eight coaches long - with a carriage washer spanning the outlet at the extreme west end of the complex. (Steam stock berthing was also concentrated by the LBSCR in Streatham, at Eardley sidings, alongside the LBSCR/LSWR Joint line south of Streatham Junction South No2.)

Streatham Hill station is set in about the centre of three-quarters of a mile downgrade at 1 in 111. Though the depot complex is not at this gradient it nevertheless is still

The 9.20 am Victoria–Holborn Viaduct service, formed of ex-Brighton stock augmented by a Bulleid all-steel trailer, passes West Norwood Junction whose signalbox roof is in the foreground. The longstanding route was Crystal Palace, West Croydon, Sutton, Wimbledon, Streatham, Tulse Hill and Herne Hill. 25 August 1956.

The Lens of Sutton Association

not completely on the level. This was starkly illustrated on 12 July 1960 when 2 BIL unit no. 2101 ran away along the up siding, mounted the buffers and finished up lying foul of the down local on the Croydon line having lost its leading bogie. (The 2 BILs appear to suffer more than any other class of unit, three sets being destroyed by enemy action and the trailers of five others being written off through accident damage.)

The goods yard, lying opposite the carriage sidings, consisted of a single road coal depot with a release loop and headshunt crammed in against three more berthing sidings making a connection into the down line at the end of the down platform. These were laid in for berthing 'overhead' stock working to Crystal Palace from the start of electric operation on 12 May 1911. But the goods yard closed prior to Mid-Sussex line electrification in July 1938 to permit reconfiguration of the area, now providing five electrified carriage sidings with access platforms between them.

Several of the overhead line gantries had survived in the sidings on the down side for lighting purposes though these were lost when the yard facilities were updated in 2005. But a long legal argument against the train operator Southern's contention that planning permission was not required for this development followed immediately, initiated by Lambeth Council, prompted by local residents. The Council eventually granted conditional retrospective planning consent in May 2012. But in view of the proximity of the site to the backs of neighbouring houses the nearest of

the covering platform canopies has had to be removed.

With the carriage sheds and sidings left behind us the four lines from the Croydon direction sweep in on the up side to make a junction at 4 miles and 69 chains from Victoria. Our route joins the local lines on the north side of the layout before coming to Balham, seventeen chains further on. Opened as Balham Hill, this station has undergone several changes over the years, mainly because of trackbed widening. The station building dating from 1862 still remains in use on the north side of the formation, just off Balham High Road which the line bridges at the up end. This is a typical two-storey redbrick structure with a lengthy glazed canopy along the road frontage to the east, and the 1926-built slab-concrete London Underground station occupying the street corner immediately to the west.

By 1868, only six years after opening, the two tracks from Croydon had been increased to three by provision of an additional up line, Balham's up platform now becoming an island. In anticipation of the continued growth in traffic the underbridge at the down end of the station had already been rebuilt to take four lines. The station was moved to its present position east of Balham High Road at that time and renamed plain Balham. The Southern Railway added the suffix '& Upper Tooting' in March 1927, presumably to differentiate it from the underground station which had opened in December the previous year: it reverted under BR to the original name in October 1969.

Despite the bridge infrastructure widening of the 1860s another three decades elapsed before another – down - line was added to the formation, in November 1895. This line ran round the back of the existing down platform which, unlike its up side neighbour, was not made into an island. Instead a new platform was built on the down side and provided with a rather mean waiting shelter. At this time and, indeed, until electrification when 'fast' and 'slow' lines were paired thus, the four tracks were paired by direction. The change may be seen in the reverse curve of the track heading away from Balham Junction towards Streatham Hill.

The most significant change to the station occurred during the spring of 1954. The main line island platform had already been renewed and slightly extended with Exmouth Junction concrete, though the timber buildings and canopy remained untouched. Some deterioration of the timber on the up local platform had also been attended to. But the unsatisfactory platform layout remained until that year when the down local platform was demolished, the track pushed over into its place after strengthening the trackbed and the up local platform widened to form an island. A new steel canopy was erected on it but to minimise weight on the embankment the timber platform was retained. The main line island platform, at which traffic rarely called in BR days, remained untouched but is now completely devoid of buildings and cover.

The first Balham signalbox stood on the south side of the incoming Croydon line though this was superseded by Balham Junction box, in a similar position though slightly closer to the station, in 1898. This in turn was made redundant with the commissioning of power signalling in October 1952 when a new box opened in the 'V' of the diverging routes. The Victoria signalling centre took over control on 7 June 1981.

The route now drops downhill at 1 in 94 to pass through Wandsworth Common (4m 5ch). This station is a relative latecomer though its predecessor on this site opened with the line but lasted for only fifteen months and then as a terminus. Being temporary it was of timber construction but the rapid development of good housing in the area saw the new station opened on 1 November 1869. By that time the three tracks were in place requiring an island platform to be constructed between the two up lines. The brick building

stood on the down side platform which had the coal yard of three sidings behind it with two outlets into the down line. The yard closed at the end of September 1964.

The signalbox straddled the up main line about five chains south of the platforms but was moved to adjoin that end of the up main platform in the 1890s, probably in anticipation of the introduction of the fourth line through the station. Being laid on the down side this line required the construction of a new two-storey station building, of rather more substantial aspect to reflect the growing status of the area, set back behind the original. The station then, as now, featured side platforms by the outer lines and an island between the up local and down main. They are joined by a covered footbridge. During the First World War a second signalbox was erected at the north end of the up main platform but never opened. As at Balham, power signalling came into operation here in October 1952.

The gradient now eases to 1 in 166 as the line bisects the common for almost three-quarters of a mile to come to the site of New Wandsworth station at three miles and nineteen chains from Victoria. This was the WEL&CPR's main station in the locality, opening with the extension from the original Wandsworth Common station to Battersea Pier on 29 March 1858. It continued to exist even after the opening of Clapham Junction on 2 March 1863. The route is in a shallow cutting here, the station being within it and located immediately south of the bridge carrying Battersea Rise over the track. Access to both the forecourt and the coal yard was from the east side of the bridge.

Unlike the passenger part of the station the yard, which contained three sidings with a short runround loop at its eastern extremity, was on virtually the same level as the road, its outlet being along a ramp of fairly shallow gradient into the down [local] line. It remained in use until 7 October 1968 though the station had closed almost a century earlier, on 1 November 1869, and was completely demolished. Oddly, it continued to appear on the LBSCR 'Table of Distances' into the 20th century as though it were still a completely functioning entity.

The station building was at the north end with footbridge access thence to the two platforms. As at Balham, the up platform was made into an island when the third line came into use in 1863. The first signal box stood

Opposite top - Norwood Junction's double-dome class 'C2X' 0-6-0 No 32543 stands proudly - and clean! - at the bay platform 5 in the original part of Crystal Palace station at the head of 'The John Milton Special'. It took the train to New Cross Gate where former 'Met' electric engines, No 2 ('Thomas Lord') and No 14 ('Benjamin Disraeli') topped and tailed the Special to Rickmansworth. Ex-Metropolitan 'A' class 0–4-4T No 81, by then renumbered L48, made a return trip on the Chesham branch before the two electric locos brought the train back over the same route through to Crystal Palace.
Transport Treasury / A E Bennett 3 June 1956.

Opposite bottom - The 'Kent & East Sussex Special', double-headed by Wainwright 'L' 4-4-0s Nos 31760 and 31768, passes Gipsy Hill signalbox. These engines took the train from Victoria to Robertsbridge via Beckenham Junction, Bromley South, Swanley, Otford, Sevenoaks, Tonbridge and Tunbridge Wells, but used the Continental boat train route from Tonbridge on the return. 'Terriers' Nos 32670 and DS680 'topped and tailed' six of the ten coaches to Tenterden and back.
Transport Treasury / R C Riley 18 October 1959.

4 SUB unit No 4626 leaves Crystal Palace working a London Bridge - London Bridge 'circular' service via Tulse Hill and Sydenham. The ridged crown of Sydenham Hill rises in the background. In the background in the 'John Milton special'.
Transport Treasury / R C Riley 3 June 1956.

between the up and down lines in the shadow of the road bridge, but the second one was on the up side close to the trailing ladder crossing at the down end of the station site. It seems likely the change occurred when the fourth line came into use. A quite magnificent set of Brighton signals for the up direction overshadowed this box, the arms at the top of the usual tall posts being fully repeated at eye level. This box was another closed on 12 October 1952.

Clapham Junction – publicly claimed to be Britain's busiest railway station - lies on a short piece of level track at the foot of the near five-mile long fall from West Norwood, immediately north of the bridge that carries St John's Hill over the line. Despite its name the station is actually in Battersea, part now of the London Borough of Wandsworth. Clapham High Street, if one counts that as the town centre, is one-and-a-half miles away to the east. The anomaly arose because at the time of opening Battersea was seen as the 'poor relation' of increasingly fashionable Clapham. The three companies whose lines met here, LBSCR, LSWR and WLER, agreed to adopt the more upmarket title, reasoning it ought to provide a greater enticement for the travelling public, especially its wealthier segments.

It is not intended to provide a comprehensive account of every change at Clapham Junction, which would demand an article and more to itself. But the major developments affecting the LBSCR side of the station will be considered. By the time it opened the three tracks of the

Brighton line between Balham and Victoria were already in use but the platform arrangement did not follow that of the two stations to the south. The up lines each had a platform but the one on the up local turned its back on the up main line while the down line shared an island platform with the up direction West London. The WLER's tracks were mixed-gauge to accommodate GWR broad-gauge traffic, that company being a party to both the West London and the West London Extension Railways. (The GWR and LNWR had half-shares each in the WLR and held one third each of those of the WLER, the remaining third being divided equally between the LBSCR and LSWR.) The junction of the Brighton and WLER routes was made at the south end though the broad-gauge curtailed progress here.

The Brighton's first booking office was located off the west side of St John's Hill in Prested Road. A subway from it provided access to all platforms, those of the other companies included, though a lattice footbridge joined the LBSCR platforms at the down end. The subway was extended in 1907 to a new entrance in Winstanley Road, at the opposite side of the station.

Two signalboxes governed movements, the first south box abutting the north face of the St John's Hill bridge but straddling both the up lines and so raised high enough for the signalman to see over it. North box stood between the Brighton down line and those of the WLER. There was, incidentally, no direct connection between the Brighton and South Western well into BR days, other than a short transfer

Immaculate 'School's class 4-4-0 No 30936 'Cranleigh' heads the Tattenham Corner - bound Royal train through Clapham Junction. A couple of surviving overhead gantries may be seen.

The Lens of Sutton Association

siding at the up end of the layout which permitted movement of vans, horse boxes and similar coaching traffic from one company to the other.

The first major change on the Brighton side occurred with the installation of the fourth line through to Balham Junction. This was authorised on 4th August 1890 and the long lead time before it opened is indicative of the complicated alterations that needed to be made both to the station directly and in its vicinity to accommodate it while still maintaining the full flow of traffic. The new line was placed on the down side, but beyond the south end of the station and the St John's Hill bridge it had to be taken through the cutting from New Wandsworth. Rather than buy up any more land on the east side – the west side is, of course, bounded by the LSWR main line - a retaining wall was constructed but with an overhanging and buttressed parapet, work being completed and track laid by the middle of 1894.

Within the station itself the additional line had to be routed to pass by the outer face of the island platform used to that time by up WLER trains. In turn the WLER down platform became an island so that that company's up and down lines were both moved the equivalent of one track eastward. These changes came into use in the summer of 1895, although the previous arrangement of other platforms remained unchanged for the moment. The south signal box was transferred to the other side of the St John's Hill bridge and, as before, stood high and straddled the pair of up tracks.

It has already been noted that the four lines were paired by direction but their use was unusual, they being respectively, from the east, Down Local, Down Main, Up Local, Up Main. Change to this arrangement in the early 1900s resulted in use being more conventional with the up and down main lines side by side to the west of the locals. However, platform use remained unchanged which meant the down main line, still alongside the narrow and spartan platform 7, was crossed over by the up local at each end of the station. This very unsatisfactory position left the Brighton with little option but to continue rebuilding, though over another lengthy period of time. When this had been completed in 1916, the WLER down line had been pushed a little further east to run alongside a new side platform. That company's up line faced an island that provided accommodation on its other side for the LBSCR down local. These three platform faces were then numbered 12, 11 and 10 respectively. The eastward move permitted the next island platform to the west to be widened, the up local being alongside its east face, No 9, while the down main used the opposite face, No 8. No 7, still serving the up main, had now become the east face of a widened island platform with the South Western's down local line opposite.

It may be noted that up to this time Clapham Junction's island platforms had always been allocated a single number, but following the rebuilding separate numbers, as already intimated, were allocated to each platform face in the Brighton and WLER parts of the station. Neither the South Western nor the Southern after it took any steps to bring the rest to conformity until

The 'South Londoner' Special stands in the up 'bay' at Beckenham Junction with an ex-SECR 'H' class 0-4-4T No 31521 providing the motive power to the two-coach 'push/pull' set made up of ex-SECR stock. The appropriate signal for the train to proceed towards Bromley Junction has been pulled 'off'.

Transport Treasury / Prof. H P White 1958.

immediately before Nationalisation when all the faces were renumbered 1 to 17 from the west.

From 1910 the LBSCR sported a very fine two-storey brick station building facing St John's Hill with a spacious cab road fronting it. From this a wide footbridge with lifts for luggage was linked to the South Western's footbridge across its main lines. Access to the whole station from the Brighton end was permitted though division remained, the bridge being split longitudinally to guide intending LSWR passengers toward that company's booking office above platform 5, otherwise reached by a long, covered footbridge from St John's Hill.

The Brighton closed the Prested Road ticket office at this time, though another was provided within the station subway. A Parcels Office was opened beneath the station building with access to a milk dock and a small yard off the WLER line through platform 12. (The South Western had its own milk dock by Platform 4.)

Electrification of the Local line trains at 6700v began on 12 May 1911. One of the two Pig Hill sidings, which lay between North box and the WLER lines descending towards Latchmere Junction and which were

directly accessible from the Local lines, was equipped with the overhead for use should emergency turnback be necessary. The Main Lines were not wired until later, though the overhead was never used in service for anything other than local work. Third rail services started on 3 March 1928 but overhead operation continued until 22 September.

The layout of 1920 remained basically unchanged for the next fifty years. Power signalling, introduced from 12 October 1952 saw the demise of the Brighton's mechanical boxes. The method of supporting the overhead wires between Clapham Junction and Pouparts Junction, where the high level approach to Grosvenor Bridge peeled away from the original line, had been unconventional and forced on the Brighton by the limited space between adjacent tracks. Massive cantilever gantries stretching over all four Brighton lines from the down side were necessary, but a few of these overhead structures were put to later use as semaphore signal gantries. They continued to support the new colour lights for many years.

A gentle down grade leads to Pouparts Junction, two miles from Victoria. It is named after Samuel Poupart, who manufactured jams and preserves from the products of the orchards he owned here. (Production was moved to Twickenham after the railway purchased the land.) At this point the four-track high-level approach to Grosvenor bridge swings away on the down side, climbing at 1 in 120 to Battersea Park station. Originally this was a double junction with the main lines but under present day arrangements the original Battersea route is accessed from a single lead off the up main preceded by a trailing crossover to permit down trains to reach the appropriate track. Double track again immediately after the divergence and heading for Factory Junction on the ex-LCDR line out of Victoria – the 'factory' was Longhedge Works – it passes beneath the four Brighton tracks heading for Battersea Park and within a hundred yards the original WEL&CPR line, now single and named Battersea Reversible, diverges on the up side. Curving sharply towards the north it passes under the South London lines and the former Chatham route as well as the seven LSWR tracks out of Waterloo. (Note that in the intervening years there have been track rearrangements in the vicinity to assist operation.) It levelled out before reverting again to the

west of the Chatham and Brighton lines. Having passed under the latter it came to the Pimlico terminus about ten chains further on. This station faced across the river some 100 yards from the foreshore and nearly 1½ miles from Pouparts Junction. Battersea Pier itself was almost underneath the west side of Grosvenor Bridge.

Two tracks passing the up side of the station turned sharply to the east, under the southern end of the bridge to lie parallel to the Thames. Two sidings diverged from this, running westward along the length of the waterfront to Chelsea Bridge, mooring posts being provided alongside them at regular intervals. By use of wagon turntables access was provided from these sidings to a two-road goods shed just north of the passenger building.

Pimlico station had a life of only 2½ years, closing on 1 October 1860, the first, adjacent, Battersea Park station having opened the day before. That station closed ten years later though the present Battersea Park had been in business since 1 May 1867. Pimlico station was subsequently used as a carriage shed and three roundhouses later superseded

The magnificent frontage of Crystal Palace station with its iron and glass 'port-cochere', and lantern roof over the booking hall. The arches of the approach road spanning the tracks are evident.

Transport Treasury / Prof. H P White 1958.

Longhedge Junction where the routes to Factory Junction and Grosvenor Bridge diverge. The latter consists of up and down lines passing directly in front of the signal box. On 26 July 1959 'Battle of Britain' class 4-6-2 No 34070 'Manston' is heading a troop train made up of Midland stock and sporting the No 19 headcode. This indicates it will travel via Maidstone East. It is apparent from its position that the train has already passed through Ludgate Junction from the Windsor side of Clapham Junction.

Transport Treasury / R C Riley 3 June 1956.

the small three-road locomotive depot lying between the viaducts carrying the Brighton and Chatham lines towards Grosvenor Bridge. The first of these roundhouses was in being to the west of the Brighton main line by 1870 though not then rail-connected.

As noted earlier the West End of London & Crystal Palace Railway was worked by the LBSC from the first, but it was the Brighton that leased it in 1858 and absorbed it the following year, though the section east of Bromley Junction to Beckenham went to the London, Chatham & Dover Railway in 1860. The Brighton opened the short spur between Birkbeck Junction and Norwood Junction on 18th June 1862. After singling and withdrawal of passenger services post-Grouping, use of the line dwindled. It closed in the early-1960s, the track subsequently being lifted and almost all the trackbed built on.

Freight traffic over the WEL&CPR route no longer features though it was once very heavy to and from Norwood where the principal marshalling yards of the Southern's Central Division were located. The yards had been developed from the late-1870s but were run down as the need for wagon sorting faded and they had closed by the mid-1980s. But some sidings in the up yard became part of the passenger rolling stock maintenance and repair depot at Selhurst. The eastern fringe of the down yard was sold for

housing though a few rusting sidings remain in the undergrowth.

The Crystal Palace & West End of London Railway continues to provide a regular passenger service through this part of the commuter belt and it is probably as comprehensive now as it has ever been. At the time of writing the off-peak timetable consists of two trains each way per hour between Sutton and Victoria via West Croydon and Crystal Palace, two Victoria-London Bridge trains via Crystal Palace and Sydenham, and two more between London Bridge and Beckenham Junction via Crystal Palace and Tulse Hill. In addition four trains per hour, operate by London Overground, work between Crystal Palace and Highbury & Islington via the Thames tunnel.

Bibliography

History of the Southern Railway, C F Dendy Marshall, rev R W Kidner, Ian Allan Ltd.,1963.
Clapham Junction to Beckenham Junction, Vic Mitchell and Keith Smith, Middleton Press, 1994.
Victoria to East Croydon, Vic Mitchell and Keith Smith, Middleton Press, 1987.
London Bridge to East Croydon, Vic Mitchell and Keith Smith, Middleton Press, 1988.
Rail Centres: Clapham Junction, J N Faulkner, Ian Allan Ltd., 1991.
London, Brighton & South Coast Railway, C Hamilton Ellis, Ian Allan

The '06' headcode shows this is a 'circular' Holborn Viaduct - Victoria service. It is seen arriving at Crystal Palace from Norwood Junction. 4 SUB No 4131 was one of two oddities formed in 1969 of motor coaches from withdrawn 2 HAL sets coupled to surplus augmentation vehicles from other withdrawn units. The photograph dates from the mid-1970s.

The Lens of Sutton Association

Ltd., 1960.

The West London Joint Railways, J B Atkinson, Ian Allan Ltd., 1984.

Railways of the Southern Region, Geoffrey Body, Patrick Stephens Ltd., 1989.

Southern Electric 1909-1979, G T Moody, Ian Allan Ltd 5th ed, 1979.

Southern Railway Handbook, B K Cooper, Ian Allan Ltd., 1982.

London, Brighton & South Coast Album, Klaus Marx, Ian Allan Ltd., 1982.

Southern Electric Album, Alan Williams, Ian Allan ltd., 1977.

Table of Distances, London, Brighton & South Coast Railway, January 1901, (Ian Allan Ltd., undated facsimile).

Pre-Grouping Railway Junction Diagrams 1914, (Ian Allan Ltd., undated facsimile).

Railway Track Diagrams No 5, Southern &TfL, Ed Gerald Jacobs, TRACKmaps, 3rd edition 2008.

British Rail – Main Line Gradient Profiles, Ian Allan Ltd., in collaboration with Tothill Press, (undated).

Streatham Guardian, Newsquest (London) Ltd., Weybridge.

South London Press, Tindle Newspapers Ltd., Farnham.

Inevitably some net searches have been made, usually to check another source or to view via Google Maps the present state of stations I have not visited personally.

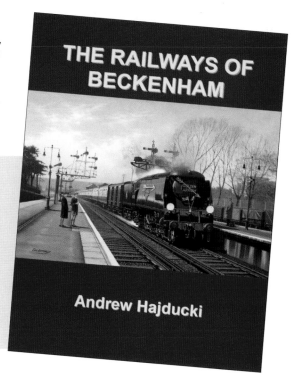

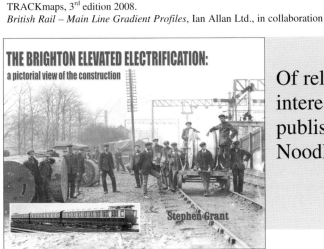

Of related interest, also published by Noodle Books.

Terry Cole's Rolling Stock File No. 27
LSWR Corridor stock

The London and South Western Railway constructed a large number of panelled corridor coaches in the early years of the 20th Century for use on its express services. However they were progressively displaced from these workings firstly by the 'Ironclads', which came into service in the 1920s, and then by an increasing number of Maunsell-designed coaches. Many were withdrawn in the 1940s, some being converted for departmental use or appropriated for ambulance trains. A few survived in service into the 1950s on excursion trains and for use on branches where the guard needed to collect fares en route.

Above - This is 080603, formerly S3090S, a 4-compartment Right Hand Corridor Brake Third seen in departmental use at Totton on 6 September 1958. It was built in June 1904 as No. 42 becoming 1318 and then SR 3090 to Diagram 138. It was withdrawn in December 1953 from set 404. The original LSWR guards' lookouts have been replaced with Maunsell ones.

Opposite top - This is 1843S, an ex-LSWR Dining Saloon, in departmental use at Lancing Carriage Works on 29 August 1959 and seen here from the non-corridor side. It was one of 23 Dining Saloons built to go with the new corridor trains. These coaches originally had clerestory roofs but they were removed by the SR in 1931. This vehicle is one of 14 which had their kitchens removed at that time and was reclassified as a 'Nonedescript' saloon, i.e. it could be used as 1st or 3rd class as needed. Many were converted for use as ambulance cars during the war or entered departmental service. I don't think this particular vehicle will be travelling far with that chimney!

Opposite bottom - Another Corridor third brake, this time no 080701 at Lancing Carriage Works on 15 August 1962. This also is the right hand corridor version but this time seen from the compartment side. Lancing was a happy hunting ground for ancient stock. The vehicle on the immediate left is a matchboard-sided ex-SECR 100 seater from the Lancing Workmens' train and to the right there is a Postal Van. [All photos David Wigley]

Moments - and the opportunity to use a couple of images that have been hanging around for a time.

Opposite is an undated aerial view of Eastleigh Locomotive & Carriage and Wagon Works. Orientated, the main London to Southampton line runs basically north-south with the Romsey and Fareham routes respectively off to the left and right. The railway houses of 'Spike Island', more accurately Campbell Road, are clearly visible. Also to be seen is the expanse of sidings on the east side of the main line, those nearest the camera referred to as Tipton yard. The vast area of the carriage and wagon works closed in the 1960s, all rolling stock work then concentrated on the former locomotive works. That too went through several name changes, 'British Rail Engineering' 'British Rail Maintenance' and after a period of almost complete closure when there was serious discussion over demolition, the site has been reborn as the privately operated 'Knights Rail Services'. Elsewhere a few of the distinctive buildings relative to the former c & w works remain, now converted for industrial use.

Above - An undated open day outside the works with No C6 and an unidentified 'Merchant Navy' attracting attention. Clearly this must be soon after 1945 (our guess is actually 1947 as malachite livery has been applied to the Pacific').

Does anyone have any aerial shots of Brighton, Ashford or Lancing, or of open days at these locations?

Unit 2070 emerging from the Brighton end of Hove tunnel. The blanking on the driver's-side window will be noted and which may then indicate wartime restrictions.

SOUTHERN RAILWAY 2 BIL UNITS
(2-car Bi-Lavatory Units)

John Atkinson with contributions from Colin Watts

Introduction

The first 2 BIL units were constructed for the 1935 extension of the Brighton line electrification to Seaford, Eastbourne & Hastings, (Ore). Order number HO 806 (dated 23 March 1934) was for ten two-coach units for the semi‑fast and stopping services. They were known as '2 BIL' units, this denoting that both coaches of the unit had access to a lavatory.

These units appeared as 1891 – 1900 although the first unit (delivered in February 1935) was numbered 1890. However, this unit was renumbered 1900 in January 1936 to make way for the final 2 NOL unit. The other nine 2 BIL units were ready about March 1935.

The 2 BIL units were ordered alongside other batches of stock for the 1935 electrification extension scheme:
6 PAN units numbered 2021 – 2037. *(Order no. HO 805 - seventeen six-coach corridor units for the express services)*
2 NOL units numbered 1824 – 1855. *(Order no. HO 807 - thirty two two-coach non-gangwayed units for local stopping services).*

This first batch of 2 BIL units (as well as all subsequent orders) was constructed at Eastleigh on new underframes from Lancing with steel‑clad timber-framed bodies and canvas-covered roofs. These units were not gangwayed between coaches and were coupled with the centre buffer /three-link chain arrangement. However, as they were intended for use on some quite lengthy services it was considered necessary for all passengers to have access to a lavatory, so each coach were provided with a side corridor and one lavatory, these being located at the opposite end to the driving cabs.

All the seating was in compartments, each compartment having an outside access door and a sliding door into the corridor. These units were equipped similarly to most of the 2 NOL units and the 4 LAV unit, (also the vast majority of the suburban three coach motor units) with electro-magnetic control equipment (supplied in this case by Metropolitan-Vickers (MV)), resulting in a large driver's cab in the motor coach and a raised floor in the guard's brake as a result of this control equipment.

However, subsequent batches of 2 BIL units were equipped with English Electric (EE) electro-pneumatic control gear (as was the last batch of 2 NOL units and all subsequent '1936 type' stock built); this equipment all being below solebar level allowing a smaller cab to be provided. This difference meant that once again and like the MV control-equipped 2 NOL units, there was a difference in the power cable conduit runs between the cab ends of the motor coach and driving trailer. The later batches had the same (driving trailer style) arrangement at both ends.

This first batch of units was regarded as satisfactory and further units of a similar type were then ordered during 1936 for the next three electrification extensions as follows:
1901 ‑ 1920 and 1954 ‑ 1971 in 1937 for Portsmouth No. 1 extension, *(Order HO 898 dated 8ᵗ January 1936 (36 units) with a further two added as order HO 903 on 27 January 1936).*
2049 ‑ 2116 in 1938 for Portsmouth No. 2 extension *(Order HO 949 dated 6 November 1938 - 68 units).*
2117 ‑ 2152 in 1939 for Reading extension *(Order HO 948 also dated 6 November 1938 - 36 units).*
The two additional units for HO 903 were added when Farnham - Alton was added to the 'Portsmouth No. 1' scheme.

SR Renumbering

The rapid expansion of the Southern Railway's electric fleet had led to the numbering system becoming rather complex, with the Portsmouth No 1 batch being split around the existing 4 LAV numbers, and a renumbering scheme was drawn up from January 1937 to tidy-up the numbers and put them into a more logical sequence, this affecting the 2 BIL units. Unit numbers 1891 ‑ 1900 now became 2001 ‑ 2010 (renumbered in order) whilst the newly delivered Portsmouth No 1 batch (not yet in traffic but in store or working running-in turns) became 2011 ‑ 2048. The final two batches of units carried their new numbers when delivered.

Changes in Design

The three larger batches of 2 BIL units had a number of detail improvements over the first ten units, principally that now having EE electro-pneumatic control gear allowed a smaller driver's cab and a larger guard's brake to be provided in the motor coaches, the luggage space in the first batch having proved inadequate. The larger guard's brake also meant that one of the full compartments in each motor coach was now reduced to a coupé (seating four) whilst the remaining six compartments were made slightly wider. Other changes were made to the location of some of the doors along the corridor side, resulting also in changes to the window layout.

Following a collision at Woking in 1937 when 2

Official view of the last of the 2 BIL sets, unit No 2152, built in November 1938 and which lasted until October 1970.

Unit No 2019 entering Surbiton in May 1952. The service is the 5.37 pm Waterloo to Ascot via Woking .

R F Roberts

BIL 2046 suffered a partial underframe collapse, the final batch of 'Reading line' units featured a reinforced underframe design and heavier buffers. This raised the buffing load from 90 to 120 tons. As a result, each vehicle in the final batch weighed about one ton more than the earlier ones.

In Service

Once delivered, this large fleet of 152 units was found working widely over all the electrified routes of both the Western and Central sections of the Southern, though they were much less common on the Eastern section, where similar duties were covered by the 2 HAL units built later for the Gillingham & Maidstone electrification scheme in 1939.

However, an eight coach 2 BIL formation was diagrammed to cover the 8.23am Sevenoaks to Cannon Street and 6.5pm return with other associated workings, the train being berthed at Orpington overnight. The train-set was changed over on Friday night, returning to New Cross Gate, with a fresh train returning to Orpington on Sunday evenings formed from a service arriving from Brighton. These workings ceased in February 1939 when new 2 HAL units took over these trains, units 2610 - 2613 being put into traffic for this working from 24 February 1939.

Formations of units up to twelve coaches long could be found from Waterloo, Victoria and London Bridge.

Units on the Central section also ran in conjunction with 4 LAV and 2 NOL units on some trains, whilst mixed formations with 4 SUB units were not uncommon. 2 BIL units also deputised from time to time on suburban services though their lower seating capacity was a disadvantage when working such trains. However, these units could not run in multiple with the 'main line' fleets of PUL /PAN /BEL and COR /RES /BUF units.

All batches of units were intermixed in traffic and units therefore received their routine maintenance at Fratton, Wimbledon Park and Lovers Walk depots. Heavier body repairs and overhauls were carried out at Lancing works whilst electrical overhauls and bogie changes were dealt with at Slade Green Repair Shop. More serious damage and collision repairs were carried out at Eastleigh works whilst other unscheduled repairs were also done at Peckham Rye and later Selhurst Repair Shops. Following closure of Lancing works in 1963, bodywork overhauls were transferred to Eastleigh.

The 2 BIL units continued on their intended duties for many years although four units were destroyed during the war by enemy action and many others suffered lesser damage. A few others with damaged driving trailers had these replaced by 'all-steel' type 2 HAL pattern vehicles during the early 1950s, some of these being mounted on recovered underframes from damaged vehicles. The toilet water heaters were isolated during the war years and not reinstated, though the hot taps remained in the toilets until removed in the early 1960s.

Nationalisation

Nationalisation in 1948 had little effect other than the units' livery changing from SR to BR green. During 1953 all units were modified with a compressor governor fitted to prevent units being able to take power until sufficient brake pressure was available to stop the train: this followed a 'runaway' collision at Guildford involving a 2 BIL unit. Similar equipment was fitted to all other units and whilst modifications were in progress a temporary restriction was imposed on two-car units running solo, and this affected unit diagrams for a while (along with those of the 2 NOL and 2 HAL units). During the modification programme, units dealt with had a small 2" diameter white circle painted on to their bodysides close to the cab doors; once all had been completed these were removed.

Third Class became Second Class in June 1956 resulting in the vehicle types changing, the motor brake third (MBT) now becoming a motor brake second (MBS).

From 1956 the 2 NOL units began to be withdrawn, their bodies scrapped and the underframes recovered for further use in the construction of new 'SR type' 2 EPB and 2 HAP units. 2 BIL units were used to cover some of the former 2 NOL duties, being supplemented by 2 HAL units now being displaced from the Eastern section by new 2 HAP units. Unit 2146 was the first to receive the new style circular BR carriage crest circa March 1957, replacing the 'riding lion' crest used hitherto.

The 2 BIL and 2 HAL units had no operational distinction (except for a small batch of 2 HAL units used between Victoria and Gatwick Airport) and were freely mixed from about 1960 onwards.

During the mid-1960s units began to gain air horns in place of their whistles and had yellow lines applied at cantrail level to indicate the location of the first-class compartments. Small yellow warning panels were painted on to cab ends from January 1964 with units 2080 and 2087 amongst the first SR units so treated, the yellow later being extended to the whole cab end. Many of the small yellow warning panels were hastily painted on (some undertaken in stabling sidings) so dates for their application are few and far between. Where a painted 'by date' is stated in the livery table (below) this may have been obtained through photographic evidence. If no date is known then N/K applies. With the yellow warning panels / ends came the black inverted triangle on the motor coaches, this donated there was no brake van at the other end of the unit.

A system of electrical code letters allocated to each vehicle was introduced in 1963 and the 2 BIL units were included in this, the motor coaches becoming CA whilst the driving trailers were DA, though the first ten units were not included in the scheme.

Corporate Blue and Withdrawal

From late 1967 units began to be repainted into BR blue livery with full yellow ends, unit 2111 being the first in October. Following the replacement of the 4 LAV units on the Brighton line in 1968/9 by new 4 VEP units, further batches of the 4 VEP units were ordered to begin replacement of the 2 BIL and 2 HAL fleet and withdrawals of undamaged units began in 1969, some still being in green livery.

The first ten 2 BIL units were among the earliest withdrawn and delivery of further 4 VEP and 4 CIG units and redeployment of 2 HAP units saw the 2 BIL fleet steadily lose the main line stopping duties on the Portsmouth line. Displaced 4 COR units were then used to replace the units on the Waterloo to Reading /Guildford lines and further 4 VEP deliveries saw the last scheduled workings on the Brighton main line on 30 April 1971,

Unit No 2037 as the lead of a brace of 2 BIL units at Angmering.

leaving their last duties on coastal local trains from Brighton.

The final day of normal public service for the 2 BIL (and 2 HAL) units was 29 July 1971 with units 2016 /2034 /2111 /2023 /2040 in use. Three units were retained for a final railtour on 25 September 1971 when the last three (2111 /2035 /2040) were withdrawn. Withdrawn units were sent to Slade Green, thence Selhurst for stripping of equipment prior to sale to scrap dealers and disposal. However, one unit, 2090, was claimed by the National Railway Museum and preserved. Unless accident-damaged, most units were withdrawn in batches and stored at various locations around the system awaiting movement to Slade Green /Selhurst for electrical stripping.

Some units were out of use for a few days/weeks prior to their official withdrawal date. Following stripping there were further periods of storage before units were hauled away to the scrap-dealer to which they had been

sold. The 'scrap date' in the following lists is usually the month in which the units were hauled away from the SR, but some survived for some time afterwards in scrap yards prior to being broken-up.

The class number 401 was allocated to the 2 BIL fleet by BR as part of the TOPS system in 1972. However, as units had all been withdrawn for disposal by this time, this was not carried on any of the units.

Units Numbered 2001 to 2010

This first batch of ten units (delivered early in 1935) was the prototype for the larger batches of units built during the next three years. Each unit consisted of a motor brake third (MBT) and a driving trailer composite (DTC), and had similar equipment to contemporary suburban units. Cab end design was similar with a domed roof and the usual side buffers, central drawhook and low level air brake hoses

	BR Liveries			
Unit	BR(S) Green Dates		BR Corporate Blue livery dates	
	Yellow warning panels	Full yellow ends	Yellow warning panels	Full yellow ends
2001	N/K	Withdrawn		
2002	N/K	Withdrawn		
2003	N/K	Yes	Withdrawn	
2004	N/K	Withdrawn		
2005	N/K	28 November 1966		
2006	N/K	Disbanded		
2007	N/K	Withdrawn		
2008	N/K	Withdrawn		
2009	N/K	11 June 1965§	Withdrawn	
2010	N/K	Withdrawn		
2011	N/K	14 August 1967§	Withdrawn	
2012	N/K	Withdrawn		
2013	N/K	Withdrawn		
2014	Withdrawn			
2015	N/K	Withdrawn		
2016	N/K	No	No	26 April 1969
2017	By June 1967	Withdrawn		
2018	N/K	Withdrawn		
2019	By 3 May 1969	Withdrawn		
2020	N/K	Withdrawn		
2021	N/K	Yes§	No	5 April 1967
2022	N/K	Yes§	No	1 June 1967
2023	N/K	Withdrawn		
2024	N/K	No	No	18 January 1969
2025	N/K	No	No	9 January 1968
2026	N/K	18 December 1967	Withdrawn	

2027	N/K	Withdrawn		
2028	N/K	Yes	No	By October 1969
2029	N/K	Withdrawn		
2030	N/K	Withdrawn		
2031	N/K	Withdrawn		
2032	N/K	No	No	By November 1970
2033	N/K	No	No	By November 1970
2034	N/K	No	No	21 July 1969
2035	N/K	Withdrawn		
2036	N/K	No	No	By October 1970
2037	N/K	Withdrawn		
2038	N/K	4 March 1968§	Withdrawn	
2039	N/K	Withdrawn		
2040	N/K	Withdrawn		
2041	N/K	Withdrawn		
2042	N/K	Withdrawn		
2043	N/K	No	No	March 1968
2044	N/K	Withdrawn		
2045	N/K	Withdrawn		
2046	N/K	Withdrawn		
2047	N/K	Withdrawn		
2048	N/K	c.May 1968	Withdrawn	
2049	N/K	Withdrawn		
2050	N/K	26 March 1968§	Withdrawn	
2051	By 1 March 1959	Withdrawn		
2052	N/K	No	No	By May 1970
2053	N/K	18 September 1967§	Withdrawn	
2054	N/K	Withdrawn		
2055	N/K	30 August 1968	Withdrawn	
2056	N/K	22 November 1968§	Withdrawn	
2057	N/K	25 August 1967		
2058	N/K	? 1967	No	9 May 1969
2059	N/K	Withdrawn		
2060	N/K	14 November 1968§	Withdrawn	
2061	N/K	Withdrawn		
2062	N/K	No	No	28 November 1969
2063	N/K	Withdrawn		
2064	N/K	No	No	5 December 1967
2065	N/K	Yes	Withdrawn	
2066	N/K	Withdrawn		
2067	N/K	No	No	By May 1970
2068	N/K	Withdrawn		
2069	N/K	Withdrawn		
2070	N/K	Withdrawn		

SOUTHERN RAILWAY 2 BIL UNITS

Contrasts in front ends. **Right -** *No 2069 is recorded departing from Crawley with the 10.36 am Victoria to Littlehampton service, 27 July 1968. The yellow panel complete with black triangle - (to indicate no brake van at the other end of the unit) was painted on this unit during March 1964. This set was withdrawn before all-yellow ends became standard on the fleet.*
J Scrace

Bottom - *'6 BIL?', three units coupled wait at Havant with a Portsmouth to Waterloo stopping service. The unit nearest the camera has yet to have roof-mounted air -horns fitted. The regulation oil tail-lamp may be noted.*

2071	N/K	Withdrawn		
2072	N/K	No	No	7 May 1969
2073	N/K	Withdrawn		
2074	N/K	4 March 1968§ (last green)	Withdrawn	
2075	N/K	No	No	By October 1969
2076	N/K	Withdrawn		
2077	N/K	Withdrawn		
2078	N/K	4 July 1967	Withdrawn	
2079	N/K	Yes	Withdrawn	
2080	N/K	No	No	6 February 1969
2081	1964	Withdrawn		
2082	N/K	Withdrawn		
2083	N/K	9 June 1965§	Withdrawn	
2084	N/K	Withdrawn		
2085	N/K	Withdrawn		
2086	N/K	No	No	By February 1970
2087	1964	Withdrawn		
2088	N/K	Withdrawn		
2089	N/K	22 October 1965§	Withdrawn	
2090	N/K	16 June 1967	No	6 February 1970
2091	N/K	Withdrawn		
2092	N/K	Withdrawn		
2093	N/K	15 November 1967§	Withdrawn	
2094	N/K	Withdrawn		
2095	N/K	Withdrawn		
2096	N/K	11 January 1967§	Withdrawn	
2097	N/K	Withdrawn		
2098	N/K	No	No	26 August 1969
2099	N/K	No	No	By June 1970
2100	N/K	Withdrawn		
2101	N/K	No	No	20 June 1969
2102	Withdrawn			
2103	N/K	No	No	By October 1969
2104	Yes	No	No	18 September 1969
2105	N/K	Withdrawn		
2106	N/K	Withdrawn		
2107	N/K	Withdrawn		
2108	N/K	Withdrawn		
2109	N/K	Withdrawn		
2110	N/K	Withdrawn		
2111	N/K	No	No	21 August 1967
2112	Yes	No	No	20 September 1968
2113	N/K	6 August 1968	Withdrawn	
2114	N/K	Withdrawn		

SOUTHERN RAILWAY 2 BIL UNITS

2115	N/K	Withdrawn		
2116	N/K	Yes §	Withdrawn	
2117	N/K	Withdrawn		
2118	N/K	Withdrawn		
2119	Withdrawn			
2120	N/K	Withdrawn		
2121	N/K	Yes	Withdrawn	
2122	N/K	Withdrawn		
2123	N/K	Yes	No	19 March 1968
2124	N/K	Withdrawn		
2125	1964	Withdrawn		
2126	N/K	Withdrawn		
2127	N/K	Withdrawn		
2128	N/K	Withdrawn		
2129	N/K	Withdrawn		
2130	N/K	10 May 1967	Withdrawn	
2131	Withdrawn			
2132	N/K	No	No	By April 1970
2133	N/K	No	No	30 November 1967
2134	N/K	No	No	By August 1968
2135	N/K	No	No	30 December 1968
2136	By February 1967	Withdrawn		
2137	N/K	March 1967	No	By June 1970
2138	N/K	Withdrawn		
2139	N/K	No	No	13 January 1970
2140	N/K	No	No	18 December 1968
2141	N/K	11 March 1967	No	30 August 1969
2142	N/K	Withdrawn		
2143	N/K	Withdrawn		
2144	N/K	Withdrawn		
2145	N/K	Withdrawn		
2146	N/K	30 November 1968	Withdrawn	
2147	N/K	16 March 1967	No	30 October 1969
2148	Yes	Withdrawn		
2149	N/K	Withdrawn		
2150	N/K	8 July 1968	Withdrawn	
2151	N/K	27 November 1967	Withdrawn	
2152	N/K	Withdrawn		

§ yellow wrap

whilst power, control and lighting jumpers were mounted on the cab end.

A standard stencil route indicator was fitted between the two cab observation lights, with the whistle to the nearside of the driver's window. The bodysides along the luggage van and cab area were not flattened and inset as on the 4 LAV units, therefore the cabs at both ends of the unit were full width. Each coach had a full-length side corridor, both these being along the same side of the unit as marshalled. When the motor coach was leading, the corridors were on the nearside.

101

Also at Surbiton in May 1952 was No 2125 on the same late afternoon Waterloo - Ascot service. (See page 95.)

R F Roberts

The motor brake third consisted of driver's cab entered by inwards opening doors each side, this cab being 9' 1" wide to accommodate some of the electro-magnetic control equipment behind the driver. Like similarly equipped suburban and 2 NOL units, this resulted in power conduits running up to roof level on the left hand side of each observation window (as seen facing the cab).

The guard's brake van followed (there was no access from this to either the cab or the passenger area of the coach), this being 7' 11¾" wide and with a pair of outward opening doors each side for access. No side lookout duckets were provided, the guard having periscopes in each direction to assist with observing signals.

The remainder of the motor brake third consisted of seven third-class compartments (all 5' 11" wide, each seating 8) giving an overall capacity of 56 third-class seats. Each compartment had an exterior access door whilst there were three doors along the corridor side. From the guard's end these were placed opposite the partition of the first/second, the door of the fourth and the partition of the sixth/seventh compartments, resulting in an outside window layout of large sidelight (L/S/L), door, three L/S/L, door, three L/S/L, door, L/S/L and toilet window.

The lavatory was located at the inner end of the coach. This coach was given the diagram number 2111 and weighed 43 tons 6cwt. The motor bogie below the driver's cab was equipped with shoegear and fitted with two MV339 motors of 275hp, though these were replaced by EE339 motors during the 1950s. Smoking was allowed in the three compartments at the van end of the coach and the two at the opposite end.

The driving trailer composite consisted of a driver's cab 4' 8⅜" deep followed by eight compartments, the four behind the cab being third-class and 6' 3" wide, the four at the inner end being first-class and 7' 1¾" wide, and finally a lavatory compartment at the inner end of the coach.

The corridor was along the offside when the cab was leading, the opposite side to that of the motor coach so that both corridors were along the same side of the unit.

Each third-class compartment again seated 8 and the firsts seated 6, giving this coach a total of 24 first and 32 third class seats. There were four access doors along the corridor side, located (from the cab end) opposite the partitions of the first/second, third/fourth, fifth/sixth and seventh/eighth compartments. There were L/S/L windows on each side of each door opening with three quarterlight windows splitting pairs of L/S/L windows along the corridor length to give a regular large/quarter/large window pattern. Each compartment again had an access door on the non-corridor side. This coach was to diagram number 2700 and weighed 30 tons 17cwt. Smoking was allowed in the two thirds behind the cab and in the three firsts at the inner end of the coach. Power conduits at this end of the unit looped up each side of the headcode glass and did not run onto the roof dome.

Overall length of the unit was 129' 5" and each weighed 74¼ tons and seated 24 first and 88 third. The non-corridor side had standard size quarterlight windows each side of the door droplight, whilst those on the corridor side were carried right up to the roofline, though the door droplights were of standard size. The passenger door droplights were to a new design with no frame, having a brass bar along the top edge and a wooden locking bar at the bottom controlled by a lever to lock/unlock them and allow the droplight to be moved. Traditional wooden-framed droplights with leather straps to control the amount of opening were retained for the guards' and cab doors. Above each passenger droplight each door had a ventilation louvre with the vent along the bottom edge. Wooden panelling in the corridor was painted cream, whilst the compartments had varnished wooden panels.

These units were ready prior to the opening of the Eastbourne & Hastings electrification scheme and were run-in on the Brighton line, indeed virtually all the diagrammed workings were on the main Brighton line as all workings east of Keymer Junction were covered by 6 car PUL and PAN units and 2-NOL units.

Four units were soon being loaned to the Eastern section until displaced by new 2 HAL units in February 1939. Once further batches of 2 BIL units were built, this batch were intermixed with them after the completion of the Portsmouth No.2 scheme and worked wherever 2-BIL units were diagrammed.

Unit 2006 was disbanded in July 1963 and used as part of a loco-hauled electrically heated set on the Oxted line, two units were withdrawn in July 1968 after exchanging their DTCs with damaged ones from later build units and the remainder in 1969 and stripped at Slade Green or Selhurst prior to sale for scrapping.

As these units were among the earliest withdrawn none received blue livery. However, units 2003/5/9/10 gained full yellow ends, those on 2009 wrapping round on to the bodysides as far back as the leading edge of the driver's door.

The following list shows unit formations with the original unit number also shown and the dates units were completed and withdrawn, also the date and location of scrapping.

Unit no. Diag no.	First no.	Unit new	MBT 2111	DTC 2700	Withdrawn	Scrapping	Scrapped by
2001	1891	Mar-35	10568	12102	19-Apr-69	Oct-69	Armytage Ltd, Sheepbridge
2002	1892	Mar-35	10569	12103	3-May-69	Sep-69	Armytage Ltd, Sheepbridge
2003	1893	Mar-35	10570	12104	26-Apr-69	Sep-69	Armytage Ltd, Sheepbridge
2004	1894	Mar-35	10571	12105	8-Mar-69	Jul-69	Armytage Ltd, Sheepbridge
2005	1895	Mar-35	10572	12106	12-Apr-69	Sep-69	Armytage Ltd, Sheepbridge
2006	1896	Mar-35	10573	12107	27-Jun-63	Feb-70	A. King Ltd, Wymondham
2007	1897	Mar-35	10574	12108 12078+	6-Jul-68	Nov-69	Bird Group, Long Marston
2008	1898	Mar-35	10575	12109 12052+	12-Apr-69	Sep-69	Armytage Ltd, Sheepbridge
2009	1899	Mar-35	10576	12110	12-Apr-69	Oct-69	Armytage Ltd, Sheepbridge
2010	1900* 1890	Feb-35	10567	12101 12129+	6-Jul-68	Nov-69	Bird Group, Long Marston

* Renumbered Jan-36
Other renumbering Jan-37

+ Later type 2 BIL DTC diagram 2701

Individual Unit Notes 2001 to 2010

2001   Unit out of use at Barnham by 30-Mar-69. Following withdrawal unit initially stored at Lancing prior to stripping at Selhurst, then stored at Balcombe and moved for scrapping 3-Oct-69 from Norwood Yard, unit arrived in yard 14-Oct-69. DTC 12102 cut-up 30-Oct-69 and MBS 10568 cut-up 31-Oct-69.

2002   After stripping, unit stored at Polegate, then Guildford and moved for scrapping 9-Sep-69 from there, unit arrived in yard 15-Sep-69. MBS 10569 cut-up 22-Sep-69 and DTC 12103 cut-up 23-Sep-69.

2003   After stripping at Slade Green, unit stored at Stewarts Lane, moving to Polegate 16-Jun-69 and moved for scrapping c22-Aug-69 from Stratford, unit arrived in yard 3-Sep-69. DTC 12104 cut-up 10-Sep-69 and MBS 10570 cut-up 11-Sep-69.

2004   After stripping unit stored at Gatwick and moved for scrapping 6-May-69 from there, train delayed at Cricklewood unit not arriving in yard until 11-Jul-69. DTC 12105 cut-up 18-Jul-69 and MBS 10571 cut-up 22-Jul-69.

2005   After stripping at Slade Green, unit stored at Stewarts Lane, moving to Polegate 16-Jun-69 and moved for scrapping c22-Aug-69 from Stratford, unit arrived in yard 9-Sep-69. MBS 10572 cut-up 12-Sep-69 and DTC 12106 cut-up 13-Sep-69.

2006   Unit disbanded 27-Jun-63 after damage repairs to DTC 12107 and both coaches transferred to set 900, later became 7 TC 701 in Feb-66. MBS 10573 operated as a trailer brake second whilst in 900/701, with motors removed. Both vehicles had their jumpers altered to allow heating from BRCW Type 3 Diesel Loco (later Class 33). Unit 701 was disbanded early in 1969 and both 10573 and 12107 withdrawn 12-Apr-69 and stored at Micheldever and moved for scrapping 31-Jan-70 from there.

2007   Unit out of use for a period in 1944 and MBS 10574 used as part of 4-LAV unit 2938, (*possibly due to war damage*). DTC 12108 badly damaged in collision with 4-SUB 4369 at Horsham 2-Jul-61 but repaired. MBS 10574 damaged by fire at Brighton 8-Jun-68, DTC 12108 to 2055 and replaced by collision damaged 12078 (ex 2055), and unit withdrawn 6-Jul-68 and stored at Micheldever then Polegate and moved for scrapping 22-Nov-69 from Gatwick.

2008   Unit involved in Ford collision 5-Aug-51 and damaged. During repairs, DTC 12109 to unit 2029 and replaced by 12052 (ex 2029). After stripping, unit stored at Stewarts Lane, moving to Polegate 16-Jun-69 and moved for scrapping c22-Aug-69 from Stratford, unit arrived in yard 3-Sep-69. DTC 12052 cut-up 8-Sep-69 and MBS 10575 cut-up 9-Sep-69.

2009   Unit out of use at Barnham by 30-Mar-69. Following withdrawal, unit initially stored at Lancing prior to stripping at Selhurst, then stored at Balcombe and moved for scrapping 3-Oct-69 from Norwood Yard, unit arrived in yard 14-Oct-69. Both coaches cut-up 29-Oct-69.

2010   This was the first built unit in February 1935 and delivered as unit 1890. It was renumbered 1900 in January 1936, and then renumbered again, along with the whole batch of ten units in January 1937, becoming unit 2010. DTC 12101 to 2096 Jul-68 and replaced by collision damaged 12129 (ex 2096), and unit withdrawn 6-Jul-68 and stored at Micheldever then Polegate and moved for scrapping 22-Nov-69 from Gatwick.

Units Numbered 2011 - 2048

This batch of units was authorised for the Portsmouth No. 1 electrification scheme and was built as unit numbers 1901 - 1920 and 1954 - 1971 but all were renumbered before entering public traffic.

Units were completed from August 1936 until January 1937 and stored on delivery, trial running commencing in February 1937. These units differed from the first batch in a number of ways, the principal difference being the adoption of electro-pneumatic control gear allowing a smaller driver's cab in the motor coach, a larger guard's brake and the reduction of the number of compartments in the motor coach from 7 to 6½. Other changes involved the door positioning along the corridor side of the trailer and consequential alterations to the window layout, flusher-fitting fixed windows mounted from the outside in aluminium frames and no ventilation louvre above door droplights.

The motor brake third consisted of driver's cab 4' 8½" deep, guard's brakevan now 11' 9½" wide, coupé compartment 4' 2½" wide seating four and six third-class compartments each 6' 3" wide. This coach seated 52 and was to diagram number 2115 and weighed 43 tons 5cwt. Motors were the EE339 275hp type from new with EE control equipment. The floor of the guard's brake van was now flat with the remainder of the coach, whilst along the corridor side, the first L/S/L before the door at the guard's end was replaced by a quarterlight, and there was no frosted glass window opposite the toilet compartment door.

The driving trailer composite had an identical internal layout to those of the first batch, one small difference being the moving of the first door at the cab end on the corridor side forwards to be opposite the doorway into the first compartment, remaining door positions being as before. The intermediate non-doorway quarterlight windows were dispensed with and the coach now had the following arrangement from the cab end, quarterlight, door, three L/S/L, door, two L/S/L, door, three L/S/L, door and quarterlight. Diagram number was 2701 and the coach weighed 30 tons 17cwt and seated 24 first and 32 third.

Overall unit length remained at 129' 5" and overall weight was now 74 tons 2cwt, whilst seating capacity was now 24 first and 84 third. The coupé compartment had the four seats facing backwards (away from the driving cab) and there was a shelf along the wall opposite, this compartment being intended for train crew travelling 'passenger' if required.

The panelling in the corridors was now varnished teak and use was made of 'Rexine', a synthetic leathercloth for other panel trim.

Units receiving full yellow ends whilst in green livery were as follows: 2011 / 2021 / 2026 / 2028 / 2038 / 2048, those on all except 2028 / 2048 wrapping round onto the bodysides as far back as the leading edge of the driver's door.

Units painted blue (with full yellow ends) were as follows:

2016 /2021 /2022 /2024 /2025 /2028 /2032 /2033 /2034 /2036 /2043.

Unit formations were as shown below, with the original unit number also shown, date of delivery, date of withdrawal and date and location of scrapping.

Unit no. Diag no.	First no.	Unit new	MBT 2115 CA	DTC 2701 DA	Withdrawn	Scrapping	Scrapped by
2011	1901	Aug-36	10577	12034	23-Jan-71	Sep-71	*Bird Group, Long Marston*
2012	1902	Aug-36	10578	12035	20-Sep-69	Oct-70	*Fratton Depot*
2013	1903	Aug-36	10579	12036	6-Sep-69	Nov-69	*Bird Group, Long Marston*
2014	1904	Oct-36	10580	12037	23-Jun-43	Jun-43	*Destroyed by enemy action Brighton*
2015	1905	Oct-36	10581	12038	24-May-69	Oct-69	*Armytage Ltd, Sheepbridge*
2016	1906	Oct-36	10582	12039	11-Sep-71	Mar-72	*J. McWilliam Ltd, Shettleston*
2017	1907	Oct-36	10583	12040	21-Nov-70	May-71	*T. J. Thomson Ltd, Stockton*
2018	1908	Oct-36	10584	12041	12-Apr-69	Feb-70	*Fratton Depot*
2019	1909	Oct-36	10585	12042	3-Jan-70	May-70	*J. Cashmore Ltd, Newport*
2020	1920	Oct-36	10586	12043	10-May-69	Sep-69	*Armytage Ltd, Sheepbridge*
2012	1921	Oct-36	10587	12044	27-Jun-70	Feb-71	*T. J. Thomson Ltd, Stockton*
2022	1912	Oct-36	10588	12045	21-Nov-70	Jul-71	*Bird Group, Long Marston*
2023	1913	Oct-36	10589	12046	13-Sep-69	Dec-69	*Armytage Ltd, Sheepbridge*

Set No 2011 at Reading General on Saturday 27 December 1969. This was one a handful of sets to receive wrap-around yellow ends (14 August 1967) but would not survive to be repainted in corporate blue. R F Roberts

2024	1914	Oct-36	10590	12047	12-Jun-71	Sep-71	A. King Ltd, Wymondham
2025	1915	Oct-36	10591	12048	23-Jan-71	Sep-71	Bird Group, Long Marston
2026	1916	Oct-36	10592	12049	4-Apr-70	Jan-71	Milton Metals, Cardiff
2027	1917	Oct-36	10593	12050	23-Jan-71	May-71	T. J. Thomson Ltd, Stockton
2028	1918	Oct-36	10594	~~12051~~ 12854 [1]	12-Jun-71	Sep-71	A. King Ltd, Wymondham
2029	1919	Oct-36	10595	~~12052~~ 12109 [2]	21-Nov-70	Jul-71	J. Cashmore Ltd, Newport
2030	1920	Oct-36	10596	12053	13-Sep-69	Oct-70	A. King Ltd, Wymondham
2031	1954	Oct-36	10597	12054	10-Jan-70	May-70	J. Cashmore Ltd, Newport
2032	1955	Oct-36	10598	12055	12-Jun-71	Sep-71	A. King Ltd, Wymondham
2033	1956	Oct-36	10599	12056	12-Jun-71	Sep-71	A. King Ltd, Wymondham
2034	1957	Oct-36	10600	12057	11-Sep-71	Apr-72	J. McWilliam Ltd, Shettleston
2035	1958	Nov-36	10601	12058	10-Jan-70	Aug-70	Armytage Ltd, Sheepbridge
2036	1959	Nov-36	10602	12059	11-Sep-71	Jan-72	J. Cashmore Ltd, Newport
2037	1960	Nov-36	10603	12060	4-Apr-70	See notes	
2038	1961	Nov-36	10604	12061	23-Jan-71	Oct-71	Bird Group, Long Marston
2039	1962	Nov-36	10605	12062	27-Dec-69	May-70	J. Cashmore Ltd, Newport
2040	1963	Nov-36	10606	12063	20-Sep-69	Apr-70	A. King Ltd, Wymondham
2041	1964	Nov-36	10607	12064	8-Feb-69	Jun-69	Armytage Ltd, Sheepbridge
2042	1965	Nov-36	10608	12065	21-Jun-69	Dec-69	Armytage Ltd, Sheepbridge
2043	1966	Nov-36	10609	12066	21-Nov-70	Jun-71	J. Cashmore Ltd, Newport
2044	1967	Nov-36	10610	12067	8-Feb-69	Jun-69	Armytage Ltd, Sheepbridge
2045	1968	Nov-36	10611	12068	21-Nov-70	May-71	T. J. Thomson Ltd, Stockton
2046	1969	Dec-36	10612	12069	10-Jan-70	May-70	Armytage Ltd, Sheepbridge
2047	1970	Jan-37	10613	12070	10-Jan-70	May-70	Armytage Ltd, Sheepbridge
2048	1971	Jan-37	10614	12071	10-Jan-70	Aug-70	Armytage Ltd, Sheepbridge

Renumbered Jan-37

[1] *'all-steel' 2-HAL DTC diagram 2705, Code DQ.*

[2] *'Early type' 2-BIL DTC diagram 2700.*

Individual Unit Notes 2011 to 2048

2011   Unit out of use at Ascot by end of 1970 and moved to Lancing for store 1-Jan-71 and withdrawn there 23-Jan-71. Moved to Selhurst for stripping 24-Apr-71, then hauled to Micheldever and moved for scrapping 8-Sep-71 from Basingstoke.

2012   Unit slightly damaged in collision in Polegate Sidings 8-Jan-63. After stripping, unit stored at Herne Hill, hauled to Micheldever 25-Jun-70 but detached at Woking after DTC 12035 damaged by fire but moved on to Micheldever by 9-Aug-70. Unit moved to Basingstoke by Sep-70 and moved for scrapping 29-Sep-70 from there.

2013   After stripping, unit stored at Polegate and moved for scrapping 22-Nov-69 from Gatwick.

2014   Coaches destroyed at Brighton by enemy action 25-May-43 and unit withdrawn 23-Jun-43 when remains of bodies scrapped. Underframe of DTC 12037 salvaged and used in construction of 'all-steel' 2 HAL DTC 12855 for unit 2700 Jun-54.

2015   After stripping, unit stored at Balcombe and moved for scrapping 3-Oct-69 from Norwood Yard, unit arrived in yard 7-Oct-69. Both coaches cut-up 16-Oct-69.

2016   Following withdrawal, unit initially stored at Lancing prior to stripping at Selhurst, then stored at Weymouth, moving to Basingstoke 25-Feb-72 and moved for scrapping 23-Mar-72 from there.

2017   Unit withdrawn 17-May-69 but reinstated from 31-May-69. After stripping at Selhurst unit hauled to Micheldever (via Eastleigh) arriving 18-Feb-71 and moved for scrapping 15-May-71 from there.

2018   Unit (with 2120) rammed by loco-hauled train at Portsmouth Harbour 5-Apr-69 and withdrawn 12-Apr-69. Scrapped at Fratton by 21-Feb-70 by France Services.

2019   Unit damaged by H/E blast at Brighton station 18-May-42 but repaired. After stripping, unit stored at Gatwick and moved for scrapping 29-Apr-70 from there.

2020   After stripping unit stored at Polegate, moving to Guildford and moved for scrapping 9-Sep-69 from there, unit arrived in yard 15-Sep-69. DTC 12043 cut-up 23-Sep-69 and MBS 10586 cut-up 24-Sep-69.

2021   After stripping, unit stored at Norwood Yard, moved for scrapping 30-Jan-71 from there.

2022   After stripping, unit moved from Selhurst to Micheldever, arriving 29-Mar-71 and stored until moved for scrapping 19-Jul-71 from there.

2023   After stripping, unit stored at Gatwick and moved for scrapping 1-Nov-69 from there, unit arrived in yard 5-Dec-69. DTC 12046 cut-up 10-Dec-69 and MBS 10589 cut-up 11-Dec-69.

2024   Unit out of use and stored at Lancing cMay-71 then moved to Selhurst for stripping, hauled to Gatwick Oct-Jul-71 for store and moved for scrapping 22-Sep-71 from there.

2025   Out of use at Ascot by end of 1970 and moved to Lancing for store 1-Jan-71 and withdrawn there 23-Jan-71. Moved to Selhurst for stripping 24-Apr-71, then hauled to Micheldever and moved for scrapping 8-Sep-71 from Basingstoke.

2026   After stripping, unit stored at Norwood Yard, moved for scrapping 5-Sep-70 from there, though not broken-up until Jan-71.

2027   After stripping at Selhurst unit hauled to Basingstoke 27-Feb-71 then on to Micheldever, 1-Mar-71 for store, moved for scrapping 7-May-71 from there.

2028   MBS 10594 damaged by fire at Waterloo Oct-66 and DTC 12051 to 2-HAL 2626 Jan-67. Unit out of use until 10594 repaired and DTC 12051 replaced by 'all-steel' 2-HAL DTC 12854 (ex 2653) from cFeb-69. Unit then 129' 6" long and weighed 74 tons. Unit out of use and stored at Lancing from 1-May-71 then moved to Selhurst for stripping 4-Jun-71 and withdrawn 12-Jun-71. Hauled to Micheldever for store and finally Feltham, moved for scrapping 15-Sep-71.

2029   Unit involved in Ford collision 5-Aug-51 and damaged. DTC 12052 to unit 2008, and replaced by 12109 (ex 2008) during repairs. Unit damaged (*where?*) cMay-66 and to Eastleigh for repairs. After stripping at Selhurst unit hauled to Micheldever 25-May-71 for store and moved for scrapping 12-Jul-71 from there.

2030   After stripping at Selhurst unit stored at Herne Hill then Battersea Yard, then moved to Micheldever 25-Jun-70 and moved for scrapping 29-Sep-70 from Basingstoke.

2031   After stripping, unit stored at Gatwick and moved for scrapping 2-May-70 from there.

2032   Unit out of use and stored at Lancing from 1-May-71 then moved to Selhurst for stripping 4-Jun-71 and withdrawn 12-Jun-71. Hauled to Micheldever for store and finally Feltham, moved for scrapping 15-Sep-71.

2033   Unit damaged mid-1962 (*where?*) and MBS 10599 damaged, repaired at Lancing. Unit out of use and stored at Lancing cMay-71 then moved to Selhurst for stripping, hauled to Gatwick 10-Jul-71 for store and moved for scrapping 22-Sep-71 from there.

2034   Following withdrawal, unit initially stored at Ford. After stripping at Selhurst unit stored at Micheldever, moving to Basingstoke 29-Mar-72 and moved for scrapping 6-Apr-72 from there.

2035   After stripping at Selhurst unit stored at Gatwick and moved for scrapping 13-Jun-70 from there, unit arrived in yard 30-Jun-70. MBS 10601 cut-up 17-Jul-70 and DTC 12058 cut-up 8-Aug-70.

2036   Following withdrawal, unit initially stored at Ford. After stripping at Selhurst unit hauled to Micheldever for store, moved for scrapping 17-Jan-72 from Basingstoke.

2037   Unit withdrawn 4-Apr-70 and sent from Norwood Yard to Derby Research Centre 25-Jul-70 as an 'Air Brake Test Unit' numbered 024. MBS 10603 renumbered DS70321, DTC 12060 renumbered DS70322. Unit withdrawn during 1972 (dumped in Chaddesden Sidings 5-Nov-72), and disposed of for scrap to Arnott Young, Bilston Apr-73.

2038   After stripping, unit spent periods in store at Three Bridges and Horsham before moving to Micheldever 29-Mar-71. Moved for scrapping 30-Sep-71 from Basingstoke.

2039   Unit damaged by H/E blast at Brighton station 18-May-42 but repaired. Unit converted at Selhurst Nov-69 for Christmas mails & parcels traffic Dec-69 prior to withdrawal 27-Dec-69. After further stripping, unit stored at Gatwick then Norwood Yard, moved for scrapping 16-May-70 from there.

2040   After stripping stored at Clapham Yard. Moved for scrapping 20-Feb-70 but train terminated at Hounslow with brake trouble and forward 26-Mar-70.

2041   After stripping at Slade Green unit moved to Gatwick for storage 23-Apr-69. Moved for scrapping 6-May-69 from there, train delayed at Cricklewood, unit not arriving in yard until 30-May-69. DTC 12064 cut-up 19-Jun-69 and MBS 10607 cut-up 25-Jun-69.

2042   After stripping, unit stored at Gatwick and moved for scrapping 1-Nov-69 from there, unit arrived in yard 5-Dec-69. Both coaches cut-up 13-Dec-69.

2043   After stripping at Selhurst unit stored at Micheldever, arriving 8-Mar-71 and moved for scrapping 27-May-71 from Basingstoke.

2044   Unit damaged in derailment at Reading cMay-66 and hauled to Micheldever 13-Jun-66 prior to repair at Eastleigh. After stripping at Slade Green unit moved to Gatwick for storage 23-Apr-69. Moved for scrapping 6-May-69 from there, train delayed at Cricklewood, unit not arriving in yard until 30-May-69. MBS 10610 cut-up 11-Jun-69 and DTC 12067 cut-up 13-Jun-69.

2045   DTC 12068 damaged in collision with 4-COR 3142 at Denvilles Jct, Havant 17-Jun-39. Unit withdrawn but reinstated cFeb-70. After stripping at Selhurst unit stored at Micheldever, arriving 2-Feb-71 and moved for scrapping 15-May-71 from there.

2046   Unit damaged in a collision at Woking in 1937 and suffered a partial underframe collapse, but repaired. Following withdrawal unit initially stored at Gatwick, moving to Selhurst for stripping Apr-70 before moving for scrapping 18-Apr-70 from there, unit arrived in yard 30-Apr-70. Both coaches cut-up 14-May-70.

2047   Following withdrawal unit initially stored at Gatwick, moving to Selhurst for stripping Apr-70 before moving for scrapping 18-Apr-70 from there, unit arrived in yard 23-Apr-70. MBS 10613 cut-up 30-Apr-70 and DTC 12070 cut-up 1-May-70.

2048   After stripping at Selhurst unit stored at Gatwick and moved for scrapping 13-Jun-70 from there, unit arrived in yard 30-Jun-70. DTC 12071 cut-up 12-Aug-70 and MBS 10614 cut-up 14-Aug-70.

Just weeks away from withdrawal, No 2024 is at Southwick with a West Worthing to Brighton service, 30 April 1971.

J Scrace

Units Numbered 2049 - 2116

This batch of units was authorised for the Portsmouth No. 2 electrification scheme and was identical to the previous batch with the exception of the final unit built. This whole batch was completed between July and December and entered service working with the earlier units. These units carried their new 20xx numbers from new.

The final unit of the batch No 2116, was experimentally built of 'all-steel' construction with steel panels welded on to a steel framework and differed slightly in appearance from the other units, particularly in the roof detail. It also had heavier self-contained buffers rather than the solid shank type fitted to the earlier units.

Units gaining full yellow ends with green livery were 2055 / 2057 / 2058 / 2065 / 2078 / 2079 / 2113, those with the yellow wrapping onto the bodyside were 2050 / 2053 / 2056 / 2060 / 2074 / 2083 / 2089 /2093 / 2096 / 2116, whilst the following were painted blue with full yellow ends: 2052 / 2058 / 2062 / 2064 / 2067 /2072 / 2075 /2080 / 2086 / 2090 / 2098 / 2099 / 2101 / 2103 / 2104 / 2111 / 2112. Unit 2074 was the last 2 BIL unit to run in green livery, being last used in April 1971.

Unit formations were as shown below with date of delivery, date of withdrawal and date and location of scrapping.

Unit no. Diag no.	Unit new	MBT 2115 CA	DTC 2701 DA	Withdrawn	Scrapping	Scrapped by
2049	Jun-37	10615	12072	23-Aug-69	Dec-69	Armytage Ltd, Sheepbridge
2050	Jun-37	10616	12073	23-Jan-71	Oct-71	Bird Group, Long Marston
2051	Jun-37	10617	12074	9-May-70	Jan-71	Milton Metals, Cardiff
2052	Jun-37	10618	12075	27-Jun-70	Jan-71	T. J. Thomson, Stockton
2053	Jun-37	10619	12076	4-Apr-70	Aug-70	Milton Metals, Cardiff
2054	Jun-37	10620	12077	4-Apr-70	Aug-70	Milton Metals, Cardiff
2055	Jun-37	10621	12078 12108 [3]	23-Jan-71	Sep-71	Bird Group, Long Marston
2056	Jun-37	10622	12079 12231 [4]	23-Jan-71	Aug-71	Bird Group, Long Marston
2057	Jun-37	10623	12080	23-Jan-71	Aug-71	Bird Group, Long Marston
2058	Aug-37	10624	12081	12-Jun-71	Sep-71	A. King Ltd, Wymondham
2059	Aug-37	10625	12082	5-Nov-66	May-67	Wimbledon Park depot
2060	Aug-37	10626	12083	4-Apr-70	Oct-70	Milton Metals, Briton Ferry
2061	Aug-37	10627	12084	4-Apr-70	Aug-70	Milton Metals, Cardiff
2062	Aug-37	10628	12085	12-Jun-71	Nov-71	A. King Ltd, Wymondham
2063	Aug-37	10629	12086	10-Jan-70	May-70	Armytage Ltd, Sheepbridge
2064	Aug-37	10630	12087	21-Nov-70	Jul-71	Bird Group, Long Marston
2065	Aug-37	10631	12088	4-Apr-70	Oct-70	Milton Metals, Cardiff
2066	Sep-37	10632	12089	9-May-70	Aug-70	Milton Metals, Briton Ferry
2067	Sep-37	10633	12090	12-Jun-71	Sep-71	A. King Ltd, Wymondham
2068	Sep-37	10634	12091	21-Nov-70	Jun-71	J. Cashmore Ltd, Newport
2069	Sep-37	10635	12092 12858 [5]	23-Jan-71	May-71	T. J. Thomson, Stockton

[3] 'Early type' 2 BIL DTC diagram 2700.
[#4] '1939 type' 2 HAL DTC diagram 2702, Code DE.
[#5] 'all-steel' 2 HAL DTC diagram 2705, Code DQ.

Unit no. Diag no.	Unit new	MBT 2115 CA	DTC 2701 DA	Withdrawn	Scrapping	Scrapped by
2070	Sep-37	10636	12093 12186 [6] 12093	4-Apr-70	Oct-70	Milton Metals, Cardiff
2071	Sep-37	10637	12094	14-Jun-69	Oct-70	A. King Ltd, Wymondham.
2072	Oct-37	10638	12095	12-Jun-71	Sep-71	A. King Ltd, Wymondham.
2073	Oct-37	10639	12096	13-Sep-69	Apr-70	A. King Ltd, Wymondham.
2074	Oct-37	10640	12097	12-Jun-71	Sep-71	A. King Ltd, Wymondham.
2075	Oct-37	10641	12098	21-Nov-70	Jun-71	J. Cashmore Ltd, Newport
2076	Oct-37	10642	12099	20-Sep-69	Dec-69	Armytage Ltd, Sheepbridge
2077	Oct-37	10643	12100	27-Sep-69	Jan-70	Bird Group, Long Marston
2078	Oct-37	10644	12111	23-Jan-71	May-71	T. J. Thomson, Stockton

SOUTHERN RAILWAY 2 BIL UNITS

2079	Oct-37	10645	12112	26-Jul-69	Nov-69	*Armytage Ltd, Sheepbridge*
2080	Oct-37	10646	12113	24-May-69	Oct-69	*Armytage Ltd, Sheepbridge*
2081	Oct-37	10647	12114	23-Jan-71	May-71	*T. J. Thomson, Stockton*
2082	Oct-37	10648	12115	9-May-70	Jan-71	*Milton Metals, Cardiff*
2083	Oct-37	10649	12116	23-Jan-71	Dec-71	*A. King Ltd, Wymondham.*
2084	Oct-37	10650	12117	23-Jan-71	Dec-71	*A. King Ltd, Wymondham.*
2085	Oct-37	10651	12118	27-Dec-69	May-70	*J. Cashmore Ltd, Newport*
2086	Oct-37	10652	12119	12-Jun-71	Nov-71	*A. King Ltd, Wymondham.*
2087	Oct-37	10653	12120	12-Sep-70	Nov-70	*J. Cashmore Ltd, Newport*
2088	Oct-37	10654	12121 12807 [7]	11-Aug-62	Aug-62	*Barnham accident (cut up on site)*
2089	Oct-37	10655	12122	11-Oct-69	Mar-70	*Armytage Ltd, Sheepbridge*
2090	Oct-37	10656	12123	11-Sep-71		*Preserved by NRM*
2091	Oct-37	10657	12124	11-Oct-69	Jan-70	*Bird Group, Long Marston*
2092	Oct-37	10658	12125	8-Feb-69	Jul-69	*Armytage Ltd, Sheepbridge*
2093	Oct-37	10659	12126	27-Sep-69	Mar-70	*Armytage Ltd, Sheepbridge*
2094	Oct-37	10660	12127	13-Sep-69	Nov-69	*Bird Group, Long Marston*
2095	Oct-37	10661	12128	4-Apr-70	Jun-70	*J. Cashmore Ltd, Newport*
2096	Oct-37	10662	12129 12101 [8]	27-Dec-69	May-70	*Milton Metals, Briton Ferry*
2097	Oct-37	10663	12130	13-Sep-69	Nov-69	*Bird Group, Long Marston*
2098	Oct-37	10664	12131	11-Sep-71	Apr-72	*J. McWilliam Ltd, Shettleston*
2099	Oct-37	10665	12132	12-Jun-71	Sep-71	*A. King Ltd, Wymondham.*
2100	Oct-37	10666	12133 12857 [9]	22-Aug-70	Dec-70	*J. Cashmore Ltd, Newport*
2101	Nov-37	10667	12134	12-Jun-71	Nov-71	*A. King Ltd, Wymondham.*
2102	Nov-37	10668	12135	4-Sep-40	Sep-40	*Destroyed by enemy action at Portsmouth Harbour*
2103	Nov-37	10669	12136	23-Jan-71	May-71	*T. J. Thomson, Stockton*
2104	Dec-37	10670	12137	12-Jun-71	Jun-72	*A. King Ltd, Wymondham.*
2105	Dec-37	10671	12138	23-Oct-65	See notes	

#6 '1939 type' 2 HAL DTC diagram 2702, Code DE.
#7 '1939 type' 2 HAL DTC diagram 2702, Code DE.
#8 'Early type' 2 BIL DTC diagram 2700.
#9 'All-steel' 2 HAL DTC diagram 2705, Code DQ.

2106	Dec-37	10672	12139	8-Feb-69	Jun-69	*Armytage Ltd, Sheepbridge*
2107	Dec-37	10673	12140	6-Sep-69	Nov-69	*Bird Group, Long Marston*
2108	Dec-37	10674	12141	2-Aug-69	Nov-69	*Armytage Ltd, Sheepbridge*
2109	Dec-37	10675	12142	21-Jun-69	Nov-69	*Armytage Ltd, Sheepbridge*
2110	Dec-37	10676	12143	7-Mar-70	Jun-70	*J. Cashmore Ltd, Newport*
2111	Dec-37	10677	12144	9-Oct-71	Feb-72	*J. Cashmore Ltd, Newport*
2112	Dec-37	10678	12145	12-Jun-71	Dec-71	*A. King Ltd, Wymondham*
2113	Dec-37	10679	12146 12196 [10] 12146	23-Jan-71	May-71	*J. Cashmore Ltd, Newport*
2114	Dec-37	10680	12147	21-Nov-70	Jul-71	*J. Cashmore Ltd, Newport*
2115	Dec-37	10681	12148	11-Oct-69	Mar-70	*Armytage Ltd, Sheepbridge*
2116	Dec-37	10682	12149	12-Sep-70	Nov-70	*J. Cashmore Ltd, Newport*

#10 '1939 type' 2-HAL DTC Diagram 2702, Code DE.

Individual Unit Notes 2049 to 2116

2049   Unit ran with DTC 12134 (ex 2101) for a period before May-55 (*reason unknown*). Unit damaged early 1960 (*where?*) and repaired at Eastleigh. After stripping, unit stored at Balcombe and moved for scrapping 18-Oct-69 from there, unit arrived in yard 1-Dec-69. DTC 12072 cut-up 6-Dec-69 and MBS 10615 cut-up 9-Dec-69.

2050   After stripping, unit spent periods in store at Three Bridges and Horsham before moving to Micheldever 29-Mar-71. Moved for scrapping 30-Sep-71 from Basingstoke.

2051   After stripping, unit stored at Norwood Yard and moved for scrapping 5-Sep-70 from there. Not broken-up until Jan-71.

2052   After stripping, unit stored at Norwood Yard and moved for scrapping 9-Jan-71 from there.

2053   After stripping, unit stored at Norwood Yard and moved for scrapping 25-Jul-70 from there.

2054   After stripping, unit stored at Norwood Yard and moved for scrapping 25-Jul-70 from there.

2055   DTC 12078 damaged in collision at Wimbledon Park 14-Mar-68 and to 2007 Jun-68. Replaced by 12108 (ex 2007). Unit out of use at Ascot by end of 1970 and moved to Lancing for store 1-Jan-71 and withdrawn there 23-Jan-71. Moved to Selhurst for stripping 24-Apr-71, then hauled to Micheldever and moved for scrapping 8-Sep-71 from Basingstoke.

2056   DTC 12079 withdrawn after collision at Brighton 31-Dec-46 and condemned 1-Nov-47. MBT 10622 spare until unit reformed with '1939 type' 2-HAL DTC 12231 (ex 2646) Nov-47. Unit then weighed 74 tons 17cwt. After stripping at Selhurst unit hauled to Micheldever 24-May-71 and moved for scrapping 5-Aug-71 from Basingstoke.

2057   After stripping at Selhurst unit hauled to Micheldever 24-May-71 and moved for scrapping 5-Aug-71 from Basingstoke.

2058   Unit out of use for a while damaged during 1957, (*details unknown, possibly derailment and sidescrape between Brookwood and Farnborough 22-Nov-56*). Unit out of use and stored at Lancing cMay-71 then moved to Selhurst for stripping and withdrawn 12-Jun-71, hauled to Gatwick Oct-Jul-71 for store and moved for scrapping 22-Sep-71 from there.

2059   Coaches withdrawn following collision with 4-COR 3135 at Wimbledon Park 20-Jun-66. Unit stripped and broken-up on site by 6-May-67.

2060   *Storage details following withdrawal unknown.*

2061   After stripping, unit stored at Norwood Yard and moved for scrapping 25-Jul-70 from there.

2062   Following withdrawal, unit initially stored at Lancing, moving to Selhurst for stripping 10-Jul-71. After stripping unit stored at Micheldever and moved for scrapping 3-Nov-71.

2063   Following withdrawal, unit initially stored at Gatwick, moving to Selhurst for stripping Apr-70 before moving for scrapping 18-Apr-70 from there, unit arrived in yard 23-Apr-70. DTC 12086 cut-up 2-May-70 and MBS 10629 cut-up 5-May-70.

2064   After stripping, unit moved from Selhurst to Micheldever arriving 2Sep-Mar-71 and stored until moved for scrapping 19-Jul-71 from there.

2065   Unit disposed of for scrap 19-Sep-70 but train delayed at Old Oak Common until 19-Oct-70.

2066   Unit withdrawn but reinstated cFeb-70. After stripping, unit stored at Norwood Yard and moved for scrapping 8-Aug-70 from there.

2067   Unit stored at Lancing from 1-May-71 and withdrawn 12-Jun-71 and moved to Selhurst for stripping. Hauled to Micheldever 24-Jun-71 for store and moved for scrapping 7-Sep-71 from there.

2068   Withdrawn but reinstated cFeb-70. After stripping at Selhurst unit stored at Micheldever, arriving 8-Mar-71 and moved for scrapping 27-May-71 from Basingstoke.

2069   Unit involved in Ford collision 5-Aug-51 and DTC 12092 badly damaged and withdrawn 22-Sep-51. MBT 10635 spare until unit reformed with new 'all-steel' 2-HAL DTC 12858, built Feb-55. Interior had EPB-style Formica and veneer finish. Unit then 129' 6" long and weighed 74½ tons, and MBT fitted with heavier buffers. After stripping at Selhurst, unit hauled to Basingstoke 27-Feb-71 then on to Micheldever, 1-Mar-71 for store, moved for scrapping 7-May-71 from there.

2070   Unit damaged (*where?*) and DTC 12093 exchanged with '1939 type' 2-HAL DTC 12186 (ex 2601) Jun-56 to Aug-57. Unit weighed 74 tons 17cwt for duration of this change. Unit disposed of for scrap 19-Sep-70 but train delayed at Old Oak Common until 19-Oct-70.

2071   After stripping at Selhurst unit stored at Herne Hill then Battersea Yard, then moved to Micheldever 25-Jun-70 and moved for scrapping 29-Sep-70 from Basingstoke.

2072   Unit out of use and stored at Lancing from 1-May-71 then moved to Selhurst for stripping 4-Jun-71 and withdrawn 12-Jun-71, hauled to Micheldever for store and finally Feltham, moved for scrapping 15-Sep-71.

2073   After stripping, stored at Clapham Yard. Moved for scrapping 20-Feb-70 but train terminated at Hounslow with brake trouble and forward 26-Mar-70.

2074   Unit stored at Lancing from 1-May-71 and withdrawn 12-Jun-71 and moved to Selhurst for stripping. Hauled to Micheldever 24-Jun-71 for store and moved for scrapping 7-Sep-71 from there.

2075   After stripping at Selhurst unit stored at Micheldever, arriving 8-Mar-71 and moved for scrapping 27-May-71 from Basingstoke.

2076   After stripping, unit stored at Gatwick and moved for scrapping 1-Nov-69 from there, unit arrived in yard 11-Dec-69. MBS 10642 cut-up 19-Dec-69 and DTC 12099 cut-up 20-Dec-69.

2077   After stripping, unit stored at Gatwick and moved for scrapping 24-Jan-70 from there.

2078	After stripping at Selhurst unit hauled to Basingstoke 27-Feb-71 then on to Micheldever, 1-Mar-71 for store, moved for scrapping 7-May-71 from there.
2079	After stripping, unit stored at Balcombe and moved for scrapping 18-Oct-69 from there, unit arrived in yard 29-Oct-69. MBS 10645 cut-up 12-Nov-69 and DTC 12112 cut-up 15-Nov-69.
2080	Unit badly damaged at Balham Jct. in collision with derailed goods train 15-May-69 and withdrawn 24-May-69. Part of bodyside of MBS 10646 torn out. Damaged unit stored at Gatwick then Guildford, moved for scrapping 9-Sep-69 from there, unit arrived in yard 19-Sep-69. MBS 10646 cut-up 3-Oct-69 and DTC 12113 cut-up 4-Oct-69.
2081	After stripping at Selhurst unit hauled to Basingstoke 27-Feb-71 then on to Micheldever, 1-Mar-71 for store, moved for scrapping 7-May-71 from there.
2082	After stripping, unit stored at Norwood Yard and moved for scrapping 5-Sep-70 from there. Not broken-up until Jan-71.
2083*	Unit stored at Norwood Yard prior to withdrawal 23-Jan-71 but sent in error on scrap train to Thomson, Stockton without stripping and still with shoegear fitted 1-Sep-71. Unit detached at Eaglescliffe and subsequently returned to Selhurst for stripping. Unit then used for accident exercises at Ashford, moving to Wimbledon Park in early April 1971 before being taken to Three Bridges for a further exercise there 12-Jun-71. Unit then moved to Micheldever for storage 26-Jul-71, and on to Feltham 16-Nov-71. Unit moved for scrapping 20-Dec-71 from there.
2084*	Unit stored at Norwood Yard prior to withdrawal 23-Jan-71 but sent in error on scrap train to Thomson, Stockton without stripping and still with shoegear fitted 1-Sep-71. Unit detached at Bedford and subsequently returned to Selhurst for stripping 20-Feb-71. Unit then used for accident exercises at Ashford, moving to Wimbledon Park in early April 1971 before being taken to Three Bridges for a further exercise there 12-Jun-71. Unit then moved to Micheldever for storage 26-Jul-71, and on to Feltham 16-Nov-71. Unit moved for scrapping 20-Dec-71 from there.
2085	Unit partly stripped at Selhurst Nov-69 for Christmas mails traffic Dec-69 prior to withdrawal 27-Dec-69. Unit further stripped and stored at Norwood Yard and moved for scrapping 16-May-70 from there.
2086	Following withdrawal, unit initially stored at Lancing, moving to Selhurst for stripping 10-Jul-71. Unit then stored at Micheldever and moved for scrapping 3-Nov-71.
2087	After stripping, unit stored at Norwood Yard and moved for scrapping 21-Nov-70 from there.
2088	Body of DTC 12121 badly damaged in collision with 2653 at Littlehampton 30-Nov-49 and withdrawn 25-Feb-50. Replaced by '1939 type' 2-HAL DTC 12807 (ex 2653). Unit then weighed 74 tons 17cwt. Underframe of 12121 used in construction of 'all-steel' 2-HAL DTC 12854 for unit 2653. Unit overturned in derailment at Barnham 1-Aug-62 when it was leading the 6-car 10:17 am Brighton to Portsmouth service. As the train entered Barnham station it derailed on the partially open switches of a facing turnout causing the left-hand wheels of the leading bogie to travel up the platform ramp, overturning MBS 10654. Unit withdrawn 11-Aug-62 and cut-up on site 22-Aug-62.
2089	After stripping, unit stored at Guildford and moved for scrapping 17-Feb-70 from there, unit arrived in yard 26-Feb-70. MBS 10655 cut-up 11-Mar-70 and DTC 12122 cut-up 12-Mar-70.
2090	Unit withdrawn 11-Sep-71 though out of use since 28-Jul-71 and briefly stored at Ford prior to moving to Preston Park 14-Aug-71 for secure storage as part of the National Collection, officially transferred 6-Apr-72. Later restored for limited use on special occasions and open days etc. Both coaches allocated numbers in the 'Private Owner' series, 10656 as NRMY 99951, 12123 as NRMY 99952, these carried on plate on underframe, original numbers still being displayed on vehicle sides. After a period in store at Lovers Walk, then West Worthing where unit suffered some vandal damage, unit moved to secure storage at St Leonards depot Aug-96. DTC 12123 moved by road to York 17-May-03 and MBS 10656 followed in June, both coaches then underwent restoration at York prior to moving to the NRM outstation at Shildon for display.
2091	After stripping, unit stored at Herne Hill and moved for scrapping 17-Jan-70 from there.
2092	After stripping, unit stored at Gatwick and moved for scrapping 6-May-69 from there, train delayed at Cricklewood, unit not arriving in yard until 6-Jun-69. MBS 10658 cut-up 30-Jun-69 and DTC 12125 1-Jul-69.
2093	After stripping, unit stored at Guildford and moved for scrapping 17-Feb-70 from there, arrived in yard 20-Feb-70. DTC 12126 cut-up 25-Feb-70 and MBS 10659 cut-up 3-Mar-70.
2094	Following withdrawal, unit initially stored at Gatwick. After stripping unit returned to Gatwick and moved for scrapping 8-Nov-69 from there.
2095	After stripping, at Selhurst unit hauled to Micheldever 8-Apr-70 for store and moved for scrapping 28-May-70 from there.
2096	DTC 12129 damaged in sidescrape collision with 4 BIG 7033 at Lovers Walk 23-Jun-68 and exchanged with 12101 (ex 2010) Jul-68. After stripping, unit stored at Norwood Yard and moved for scrapping Sep-May-70 from there.
2097	After stripping, unit stored at Gatwick and moved for scrapping 8-Nov-69 from there.
2098	MBS 10664 damaged in collision with a van train at Hove 2-Nov-49. Unit withdrawn but reinstated cFeb-70. Following withdrawal unit initially stored at Ford and after stripping at Selhurst stored at Micheldever, moving to Basingstoke 29-Mar-72. Moved for scrapping 6-Apr-72 from there.
2099	Unit stored at Lancing from 1-May-71 and withdrawn 12-Jun-71 and moved to Selhurst for stripping. Hauled to Micheldever 24-Jun-71 for store and moved for scrapping 7-Sep-71 from there.
2100	Unit involved in Ford collision 5-Aug-51 and DTC 12133 badly damaged and withdrawn 22-Sep-51. MBT 10666 spare until unit reformed with new 'all-steel' 2 HAL DTC 12857, built Feb-55. Interior had EPB-style Formica and veneer finish. Unit then 129' 6" long and weighed 74½ tons and MBT fitted with heavier buffers. Underframe of 12133 used in construction of 'all-steel' 2-HAL DTC 12856 for unit 2133. After stripping, unit stored at Norwood Yard and moved for scrapping 5-Dec-70 from there.

2101   DTC 12134 used for a period prior to May-55 in unit 2049 (*reason unknown*). Unit 'ran away' at Streatham Hill and in collision with buffers near Balham 12-Jul-63 and badly damaged, but repaired at Eastleigh May-64 after a period of storage at Micheldever. Following withdrawal, unit initially stored at Lancing and moved to Selhurst for stripping 24-Jul-71. After stripping unit stored at Micheldever and moved for scrapping 3-Nov-71

2102   Both coaches destroyed by enemy action at Portsmouth Harbour 12-Aug-40 and unit withdrawn 4-Sep-40. Underframes scrapped at Lancing during 1943, that of 10668 30-Jun-43.

2103   Unit in collision with 4-SUBs 4717 and 4703 at Wimbledon Park 24-Nov-70 and DTC 12136 cab damaged and unit withdrawn 23-Jan-71 and hauled to Micheldever 5-Feb-71 for store and moved for scrapping 15-May-71 from there.

2104   Following withdrawal, unit initially stored at Gatwick and after stripping returned there for storage prior to moving to Weymouth 25-Mar-72 and later back to Brockenhurst. Unit moved for scrapping from there 12-Jun-72 but train delayed at Hounslow and forward from there 20-Jun-72.

2105   Unit in collision with 'Queen Mary' bus on Roundstone Level Crossing (near Worthing) 22-Aug-65 and DTC 12138 derailed and damaged by fire and withdrawn 23-Oct-65. Body of 12138 scrapped at Brighton Nov-65. MBS 10671 to store at Micheldever 5-Dec-65 until Nov-66 then to 4-LAV 2943. Underframe of 12138 also stored at Micheldever with 10671, (*eventual disposal unknown*).

2106   After stripping, unit stored at Gatwick and moved for scrapping 6-May-69 from there, train delayed at Cricklewood, unit not arriving in yard until 6-Jun-69. MBS 10672 cut-up 23-Jun-69 and DTC 12139 cut-up 27-Jun-69.

2107   After stripping, unit stored at Polegate and later Gatwick and moved for scrapping 22-Nov-69 from there.

2108   After stripping, unit stored at Gatwick and moved for scrapping 11-Oct-69 from there, unit arrived in yard 22-Oct-69. DTC 12141 cut-up 1-Nov-69 and MBS 10674 cut-up 5-Nov-69.

2109   After stripping, unit stored at Gatwick and moved for scrapping 11-Oct-69 from there, unit arrived in yard 22-Oct-69. DTC 12142 cut-up 13-Nov-69 and MBS 10675 cut-up 11-Nov-69.

2110   After stripping at Selhurst unit hauled to Micheldever 8-Apr-70 for store and moved for scrapping 28-May-70 from there.

2111   Unit retained after units withdrawn 29-Jul-71 to work final railtour 25-Sep-71 then withdrawn and after stripping at Selhurst stored at Shalford from 13-Jan-72. Moved for scrapping 11-Feb-72 from there.

2112   Following withdrawal unit stored initially at Lancing and moved to Selhurst for stripping 9-Sep-71. Stored (*probably at Norwood Yard*) and moved for scrapping Dec-71.

2113   Unit in collision with 2-HAL 2611 at Wimbledon Park late 1959 and MBS 10679 damaged. DTC 12146 exchanged with damaged 12196 (ex 2611) and unit stored at Hassocks prior to repair at Lancing. Reverted to original formation Mar-61. Unit weighed 74 tons 17cwt for duration of this change. After stripping at Selhurst unit hauled to Micheldever arriving 8-Mar-71 and moved for scrapping 8-May-71 from there.

2114   Following withdrawal, unit stored initially at Lancing. After stripping at Selhurst unit hauled to Micheldever 25-May-71 for store and moved for scrapping 12-Jul-71 from there.

2115   After stripping, unit stored at Guildford and moved for scrapping 17-Feb-70 from there, unit arrived in yard 26-Feb-70. DTC 12148 cut-up 7-Mar-70 and MBS 10681 cut-up 14-Mar-70.

2116   After stripping, unit stored at Norwood Yard and moved for scrapping 21-Nov-70 from there.

* Readers will note some similarity in the disposal history of these two units which may be explained thus. The first unit was dropped at Bedford although the reason is not stated. It could well have been due to a hotbox or one of the shoebeams sustaining damage (they were not removed for transit!).

Units Numbered 2117 - 2152

This final batch of thirty-six 2 BIL units was authorised for the extension of electrification from Virginia Water to Reading (Southern), Ascot to Ash Vale and Aldershot (South Junction) to Guildford. This scheme covered 88 track miles and also included electrifying the local lines between Pirbright Junction and Sturt Lane Junction and round the spur to Frimley Junction though these lines were not used by regular timetabled electric trains.

Engineering work for this scheme was less extensive than that required for both the Portsmouth schemes, it involved lengthening platforms to 540' where necessary, a new goods yard was provided at Virginia Water as a consequence of track layout alterations there.

At Ascot there were separate platforms for the Reading and Guildford lines and a new spur was provided at the west end of the station to allow the splitting of electric trains there for both routes. This required the provision of a new signal box and the new arrangements being brought into use from 16 October 1938.

Berthing sidings were provided at Reading and additional sidings electrified at Guildford. Power supplies for this scheme saw current taken from the CEGB at Reading and distributed to ten rectifier substations, six of these between Virginia Water and Reading, three between Ascot and Ash Vale and one between Aldershot and Guildford. These were controlled from the existing control room at Woking.

Trial running of electric trains began from 30 October 1938, though a unit had been steam-hauled to Reading on 23 October for shoe clearance trials, and the full public service commenced from 1 January 1939 although the official opening had taken place on 30 December 1938 when a 4 BUF unit ran from Waterloo to Reading picking up Mayors, Town Clerks and other civic leaders en route.

The train service consisted of trains at ½-hourly frequency running fast from Waterloo to Staines and dividing at Ascot for Reading & Guildford, the Guildford portion reversing at Aldershot. In busy hours the frequency stepped up to every twenty minutes and there were a few trains from Ascot to Woking via Aldershot with London connections to avoid Camberley line passengers having to change at Ash Vale.

Units 2117 - 2152 provided for this scheme were delivered from July to November 1938 and the bodies were identical to those of the previous two batches of units. This batch however had the stronger underframes and heavier self-contained buffers and each vehicle was heavier, the MBTs now weighing 44 tons 8cwt and the DTCs 31 tons 13cwt giving a revised unit total of 76 tons.

Units gaining full yellow ends with green livery were 2137 / 2151 whilst units 2121 / 2130 / 2141 / 2146 /2147 / 2150 were similarly treated though with the yellow wrapping round onto the bodysides back as far as the leading edge of the driver's door.

The following units were painted blue with full yellowends 2123 / 2132 / 2133 /2134 / 2135 / 2137 /2139 / 2140 / 2141 / 2147.

Unit formations were as shown below with date of delivery, date of withdrawal and date and location of scrapping.

Unit no. Diag no.	Unit new	MBT 2115 CA	DTC 2701 DA	Withdrawn	Scrapping	Scrapped by
2117	Aug-38	10683	12150	12-Sep-70	Nov-70	J. Cashmore Ltd, Newport
2118	Aug-38	10684	12151	27-Dec-69	May-70	Milton Metals, Briton Ferry
2119	Aug-38	10685	12152	13-Jan-45	Jan-45	Destroyed by enemy action (V2) at Peckham Rye depot
2120	Aug-38	10686	12153	12-Apr-69	Feb-70	Fratton Depot
2121	Aug-38	10687	12154	2-Aug-69	Feb-70	Fratton Depot
2122	Aug-38	10688	12155	8-Feb-69	Jul-69	Armytage Ltd, Sheepbridge
2123	Aug-38	10689	12156 12193 [11]	11-Sep-71	Mar-72	J. McWilliam Ltd, Shettleston
2124	Sep-38	10690	12157	12-Sep-70	Nov-70	J. Cashmore Ltd, Newport

[11] '1939 type' 2-HAL DTC diagram 2702, Code DE

2125	Sep-38	10691	12158	2-Aug-69	Dec-69	Armytage Ltd, Sheepbridge
2126	Sep-38	10692	12159	13-Sep-69	Nov-69	Bird Group, Long Marston
2127	Sep-38	10693	12160	20-Sep-69	Nov-69	Bird Group, Long Marston
2128	Sep-38	10694	12161	11-Oct-69	Jan-70	Bird Group, Long Marston

Opposite - *Unit 2139 leads the 2.30 pm Brighton to Littlehampton service at Shoreham-by-Sea on 28 April 1971. Full yellow ends and corporate blue livery.*

J Scrace

2129	Sep-38	10695	12162	26-Jul-69	Nov-69	*Armytage Ltd, Sheepbridge*
2130	Sep-38	10696	12163	23-Jan-71	Jul-71	*Bird Group, Long Marston*
2131	Sep-38	10697	12164	4-Sep-40	Sep-40	*Destroyed by enemy action at Portsmouth Harbour*
2132	Sep-38	10698	12165	12-Jun-71	Sep-71	*A. King Ltd, Wymondham*
2133	Sep-38	10699	12166 12856 [12]	12-Jun-71	Dec-71	*A. King Ltd, Wymondham*
2134	Sep-38	10700	12167	4-Jul-70	Dec-70	*J. Cashmore Ltd, Newport*
2135	Sep-38	10701	12168	9-Oct-71	Feb-72	*J. Cashmore Ltd, Newport*
2136	Sep-38	10702	12169	9-May-70	Jan-71	*Milton Metals, Cardiff*
2137	Oct-38	10703	12170	12-Jun-71	Dec-71	*A. King Ltd, Wymondham*
2138	Oct-38	10704	12171	18-Oct-69	Jan-70	*Bird Group, Long Marston*
2139	Oct-38	10705	12172	12-Jun-71	Dec-71	*A. King Ltd, Wymondham*
2140	Oct-38	10706	12173	9-Oct-71	Feb-72	*J. Cashmore Ltd, Newport*
2141	Oct-38	10707	12174	12-Jun-71	Dec-71	*A. King Ltd, Wymondham*
2142	Oct-38	10708	12175	10-May-69	Sep-69	*Armytage Ltd, Sheepbridge*
2143	Oct-38	10709	12176	26-Jul-69	Nov-69	*Armytage Ltd, Sheepbridge*
2144	Oct-38	10710	12177	11-Oct-69	Feb-70	*Armytage Ltd, Sheepbridge*
2145	Oct-38	10711	12178	10-Jan-70	May-70	*J. Cashmore Ltd, Newport*
2146	Nov-38	10712	12179	23-Jan-71	Jul-71	*Bird Group, Long Marston*
2147	Nov-38	10713	12180	12-Jun-71	Nov-71	*A. King Ltd, Wymondham*
2148	Nov-38	10714	12181	3-May-69	Oct-69	*Armytage Ltd, Sheepbridge*
2149	Nov-38	10715	12182	11-Oct-69	Jan-70	*Bird Group, Long Marston*
2150	Nov-38	10716	12183	21-Nov-70	Aug-71	*Bird Group, Long Marston*
2151	Nov-38	10717	12184	4-Apr-70	Oct-70	*Milton Metals, Cardiff*
2152	Nov-38	10718	12185	4-Apr-70	Oct-70	*Milton Metals, Cardiff*

[12] 'All-steel' 2-HAL DTC diagram 2705, Code DQ.

Individual Unit Notes 2049 to 2116

2117   After stripping, unit stored at Norwood Yard and moved for scrapping 21-Nov-70 from there.

2118   Unit partly stripped at Selhurst Nov-69 for Christmas mails and parcels traffic Dec-69 prior to withdrawal 27-Dec-69. Unit stored partly stripped at Balcombe until moved to Selhurst for further stripping, then stored at Norwood Yard until moved for scrapping Sep-May-70 from there.

2119   Unit wrecked by enemy action during V2 hit at Peckham Rye Depot 6-Jan-45 and withdrawn 13-Jan-45. Underframe of DTC 12152 used in repair of '1939 type' 2-HAL DTC 12191 in unit 2606.

2120   Unit (with 2018) rammed by loco-hauled train at Portsmouth Harbour 5-Apr-69 and withdrawn 12-Apr-69. Scrapped at Fratton by 21-Feb-70 by France Services.

2121   Unit damaged in collision with 4-CIG 7309 in Three Bridges Sidings c1-Aug-69 and withdrawn 2-Aug-69. Unit stored in disused MPD until taken to Fratton for scrapping by 21-Feb-70 by France Services.

2122   Unit damaged Feb-69 (*location unknown*) and withdrawn 8-Feb-69. After stripping, unit stored at Gatwick and moved for scrapping 6-May-69 from there, train delayed at Cricklewood, unit not arriving in yard until 11-Jul-69. DTC 12155 cut-up 17-Jul-69 and MBS 10688 cut-up 24-Jul-69.

2123   DTC 12156 damaged (*where?*) and withdrawn 3-Jan-68 and replaced by '1939 type' 2-HAL DTC 12193 (ex 2608). 12156 scrapped at A King Ltd, Wymondham Sep-68 formed as part of 4-LAV 2941. Following withdrawal unit initially stored at Lancing prior to stripping at Selhurst, then stored at Weymouth, moving to Basingstoke 25-Feb-72 and moved for scrapping 23-Mar-72 from there.

2124   Unit withdrawn but reinstated cFeb-70. After stripping, unit stored at Norwood Yard and moved for scrapping 21-Nov-70 from there.

2125   After stripping, unit stored at Gatwick and moved for scrapping 11-Oct-69 from there, unit arrived in yard 25-Nov-69. DTC 12158 cut-up 28-Nov-69 and MBS 10691 cut-up 2-Dec-69.

2126   After stripping, unit stored at Gatwick and moved for scrapping 8-Nov-69 from there.

2127   After stripping, unit stored at Gatwick and moved for scrapping 8-Nov-69 from there.

2128   After stripping, unit stored at Gatwick and moved for scrapping 24-Jan-70 from there.

2129   After stripping, unit stored at Balcombe and moved for scrapping 18-Oct-69 from there, unit arrived in yard 4-Nov-69. DTC 12162 cut-up 20-Nov-69 and MBS 10695 cut-up 26-Nov-69.

2130   Unit out of use from cSep-57 to cJun-58 damaged, (*details unknown*). After stripping at Selhurst, unit hauled to Micheldever for store, arriving 29-Mar-71 and moved for scrapping 19-Jul-71 from there.

2131   Both coaches destroyed by enemy action at Portsmouth Harbour 12-Aug-40 and unit withdrawn 4-Sep-40. Underframes scrapped at Lancing during 1943, that of 10697 23-Jun-43 and that of 12164 18-Aug-43.

One of the very first batch of 2 BIL sets which entered service in March 1935. It would have a working life of 34 years. The unit is seen inside the works at Lancing in the early 1960s with panelling removed, allowing a glimpse of the timber framing. Air horns have yet to be fitted. Note also the destination board on the side panel.

Tim Stubbs

2132	Unit stored at Lancing from 1-May-71 and withdrawn 12-Jun-71 and moved to Selhurst for stripping. Hauled to Micheldever 24-Jun-71 for store and moved for scrapping 7-Sep-71 from there.
2133	Unit in 'runaway' collision with Light Engine 30693 at Guildford 8-Nov-52 following compressor failure. DTC 12166 badly damaged and withdrawn 15-Nov-52. MBS 10699 spare until unit reformed with new 'all-steel' 2-HAL DTC 12856 built Feb-55 on underframe of former 12133 (ex 2100). Interior had EPB-style Formica and veneer finish. Unit then 129' 6" long and weighed 75 tons. After withdrawal, unit initially stored at Lancing, moving to Selhurst 17-Jul-71 for stripping. Unit then stored at Micheldever and later Feltham. Moved for scrapping 20-Dec-71 from there.
2134	Unit out of use from 4-Jul-70 and initially stored at Ford and moved to Selhurst for stripping 21-Aug-70 and withdrawn. After stripping, unit stored at Norwood Yard and moved for scrapping 5-Dec-70 from there.
2135	Unit retained after units withdrawn 29-Jul-71 to work final railtour 25-Sep-71 then withdrawn and after stripping at Selhurst stored Weymouth, moving to Shalford from 28-Jan-72. Moved for scrapping 11-Feb-72 from there.
2136	Unit withdrawn but reinstated cFeb-70. After stripping unit stored at Norwood Yard and moved for scrapping 5-Sep-70 from there. Not broken-up until Jan-71.
2137	After withdrawal, unit initially stored at Lancing, moving to Selhurst 17-Jul-71 for stripping. Unit then stored at Micheldever and later Feltham. Moved for scrapping 20-Dec-71 from there.
2138	After stripping, unit stored at Herne Hill and moved for scrapping 17-Jan-70 from there.
2139	Following withdrawal, unit stored initially at Lancing and moved to Selhurst for stripping 9-Sep-71. Stored (*probably at Norwood Yard*) and moved for scrapping Dec-71.
2140	Unit retained after units withdrawn 29-Jul-71 to work final railtour 25-Sep-71 then withdrawn and after stripping at Selhurst stored at Shalford from 13-Jan-72. Moved for scrapping 11-Feb-72 from there.
2141	After withdrawal, unit initially stored at Lancing, moving to Selhurst 17-Jul-71 for stripping. Unit then stored at Micheldever and later Feltham. Moved for scrapping 20-Dec-71 from there.
2142	After stripping, unit stored at Polegate then Guildford and moved for scrapping 9-Sep-69 from there, unit arrived in yard 11-Sep-69. DTC 12175 cut-up 17-Sep-69 and MBS 10708 cut-up 20-Sep-69.
2143	After stripping unit stored at Gatwick and moved for scrapping 11-Oct-69 from there, unit arrived in yard 4-Nov-69. MBS 10709 cut-up 20-Nov-69 and DTC 12176 cut-up 26-Nov-69.
2144	After stripping, unit stored at Guildford and moved for scrapping 17-Feb-70 from there, unit arrived in yard 20-Feb-70. DTC 12177 cut-up 5-Mar-70 and MBS 10710 cut-up 10-Mar-70.
2145	Unit hit by enemy incendiaries at Fratton Depot 3-May-41 and DTC 12178 badly burnt out but repaired. Unit damaged by enemy action at Brighton 25-May-43, MBT 10711 badly affected. Unit repaired at Lancing by 5-Oct-43. After stripping, unit stored at Gatwick and moved for scrapping 2-May-70 from there.
2146	After stripping at Selhurst unit hauled to Micheldever for store, arriving 5-Apr-71 and moved for scrapping 26-Jul-71 from there.
2147	Following withdrawal unit initially stored at Lancing, moving to Selhurst Oct-Jul-71 for stripping. After stripping unit stored at Micheldever and moved for scrapping 3-Nov-71.
2148	Unit damaged in sidescrape incident (*where?*) and at Lancing for repair Aug-64. Following withdrawal, unit initially stored at Gatwick. After stripping at Slade Green unit stored at Stewarts Lane, moving to Polegate 16-Jun-69, then Guildford and moved for scrapping 9-Sep-69 from there, unit arrived in yard 7-Oct-69. MBS 10714 cut-up 19-Oct-69 and DTC 12181 cut-up 20-Oct-69.
2149	After stripping, unit stored at Herne Hill and moved for scrapping 17-Jan-70 from there.
2150	After stripping, unit hauled to Micheldever 24-May-71 and moved for scrapping 5-Aug-71 from Basingstoke.
2151	Unit disposed of for scrap 19-Sep-70 but train delayed at Old Oak Common until 19-Oct-70.
2152	Following withdrawal, unit initially stored at Lancing, moving to Selhurst for stripping 31-Jul-70. Unit disposed of for scrap 19-Sep-70 but train delayed at Old Oak Common until 19-Oct-70.

In the eyes of many the 2 BIL sets suited green far more than corporate blue, the latter seeming to make them appear dated. To conclude then, three images in that favoured green livery. **Opposite page -** *The 6.27 pm Waterloo to Alton / Portsmouth & Southsea trains passing New Malden on 4 February 1967. The train will divide at Woking.* **Above** *- A Portsmouth & Southsea service at Esher on 12 February 1967.* **Bottom -** *Unit No 2002 (DMBT No S1211035) at Waterloo on 2 November 1966.*

All R F Roberts

(EARLY) CLOSED LINES - 2
Kensington - Shepherds Bush LSWR

An occasional feature on long-forgotten Southern area lines - and not those closed by a certain 'Dr'! Instead these are routes and stations which were deemed superfluous decades before, part of which route of infrastructure might still be traced.

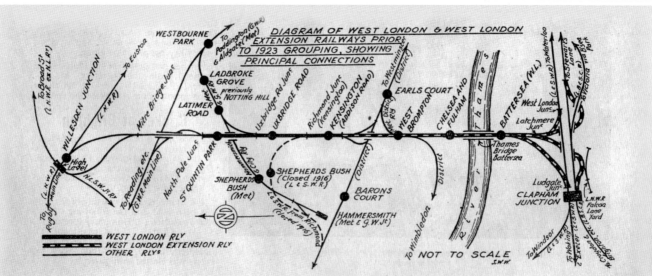

The LSWR railway through Shepherds Bush opened on 1 January 1869 - the station seen coming into use on 1 May 1874 - part of a 'blocking' line built from the WLER via Hammersmith Grove Road station and thence via existing metals to Turnham Green and eventually Richmond. The raison d'être for its existence came from a desire by the LSWR to maintain a monopoly of traffic to Richmond. Traffic was handled by both the LSWR and Metropolitan District railway and is reported to have carried some 54,000 passengers in its first month.

Shepherds Bush station was in a cutting on the west side of Shepherds Bush Road, access to the platforms being via covered steps leading down from the roadway. There were no separate goods facilities but as can be seen, signalling was provided on what was a double-track line. With electrification and in consequence competition from the neighbouring Metropolitan lines together with its neighbours, traffic dwindled and the station, indeed the route itself, was closed from Monday 5 June 1916.

The route and its infrastructure remained in what was effectively limbo until 1926 when the SR board authorised the recovery of the permanent way at least and signalling. Even so, and as seen by the date of the accompanying images, that at Shepherd Bush was still intact more than two years later.

A decade later, in 1937, building work on the east side of the station effectively blocked the trackbed, subsequent to which further industrial and domestic construction has removed most traces, although the platform and the site of the overbridge at the station may still be found.

Opposite - *The station and signal cabin looking east from the ground, this time on 29 August 1928.*

Above - *Shepherds Bush Station looking east from the down starting signal, 7 September 1928. Weeds are obvious, after all there had been no trains for over 12 years, but what is also apparent is the lack of vandalism. A board crossing at the end of the platforms may just be discerned.*

Both images from the David Wallis collection.

A sunny day in June 1962 sees No 34022 'Exmoor' waiting departure from Brockenhurst -Bournemouth bound.

Roger Holmes